WHY WOMEN WORRY

...and
How to Stop

WHY WOMEN WORRY

...and
How to Stop

JANE AND ROBERT HANDLY
WITH
PAULINE NEFF

PRENTICE
HALL
PRESS

NEW YORK/LONDON/TORONTO
SYDNEY/TOKYO/SINGAPORE

Where case studies appear, names, professions, locations, and other biographical details about the people have been changed to preserve their privacy and anonymity. The information in this book is not intended to replace the services of a qualified professional. If you know or suspect that you have a particular problem described in this book, you should consult a professional.

Prentice Hall Press
15 Columbus Circle
New York, New York 10023

Copyright © 1990 by Prentice Hall Press

PRENTICE HALL PRESS and colophons are registered trademarks of Simon & Schuster, Inc.

Library of Congress Cataloging-in-Publication Data

Handly, Jane.
    Why women worry—and how to stop / Jane and Robert Handly with Pauline Neff.
        p.   cm.
    ISBN 0-13-957267-8
    1. Women—Psychology.   2. Worry.   3. Self-help techniques.
    I. Handly, Robert.   II. Neff, Pauline.   III. Title.
    HQ1206.H239   1990
    155.6'33—dc20   90-33241
                                                                       CIP

Designed by Robert Bull Design

Manufactured in the United States

10 9 8 7 6 5 4 3 2 1

First Edition

To our family and friends,
whose loving support
we greatly value.

ACKNOWLEDGMENTS

◆ ◆ ◆

We wish to acknowledge the following friends and associates for helping us compile and edit the information that was gathered in preparing this book. We especially thank Eileen McDargh, Susan Roane, Dorothy Fischer, and Cynthia Handly for coordinating focus groups, and also the many women who shared their personal experiences in dealing with worry.

We gratefully acknowledge the contribution of Jim Wilson in helping us deal with and understand the psychological components of worry.

We thank Pauline Neff for her extraordinary talent and patience in helping us to put into print our thoughts, ideas, and experiences.

We acknowledge Toni Sciarra for her expert editorial advice.

CONTENTS

◆ ◆ ◆

I have known a great many troubles
but most of them never happened.

—Mark Twain

PART I

$\bullet\ \blacklozenge\ \bullet$

What Causes Worry?

CHAPTER 1

♦ ♦ ♦

The Worry Trap

You wake at 3 A.M. worrying about money. If you don't pay the rent tomorrow, you will be penalized. If you do, you can't write a check for the credit card bill. Just like last month, you'll be socked with 18 percent interest. Why can't you ever get out of debt? What's wrong with you? Good-bye, sleep! Hello to another red-eyed morning.

Or you're worrying about getting fat. How will anyone love you if you're overweight? When you watch television it seems that every female besides you wears a size eight. Miserable, you open another bag of chips.

Or you're worried about the hostility and bad grades of your teenagers. Could they be on drugs? You picture them in trouble with the police, in prison, or lying dead from an overdose. Your stomach starts to hurt. How are you going to do your work with family worries weighing so heavily on your mind? Already the office is abuzz with talk about putting women with children on the "mommy track." What will you do if you get passed over for that promotion you wanted? Every time you think about it you get a headache.

Or you're worried about having enough energy to balance your responsibilities between your hospitalized father and your family. After battling rush hour traffic to reach the hospital after work, you can barely muster a smile for the patient. In return your Dad complains, "My roommate's daughter has been here all day." How can you convince him that you really care? Meanwhile, who's going to make dinner for your spouse, your grown son, and the grandchildren who have moved back in with you? Your heart starts pounding when you catch a glimpse of your watch. You'll never be adequate or strong enough to do everything you need to do.

Worry. As a female, you probably know that feeling of distress and agitation over future events. What if you fail? What if you are rejected? Negative thoughts and visions of yourself doing exactly what you don't want to do keep breaking into your awareness, and you can't seem to stop them. Strangely, you feel that if you just worry enough, these bad things won't happen to you; but at the pit of your stomach (which is already in knots) you're sure that they will.

Worry researchers Janet M. Stavosky and Thomas D. Borkovec of the Pennsylvania State University define worry as a series of negative thoughts and images that intrude into awareness in an uncontrolled manner. Worriers are those people who report worrying 50 percent or more of each day and feel that it is a problem for them. According to their study, published in the fall 1987 volume of *Women & Therapy*, Stavosky and Borkovec report women are worriers at a rate of two to three times that of men. This is not to say that men do not worry—they do. However, among the 13 million people in the United States affected by phobias and related anxiety disorders (such as panic attacks and panic and/or anxiety disorder), the National Institutes of Mental Health report that far more of them are women. Women also report more psychological difficulties and are diagnosed as having disturbances more frequently than males.

Granted, women more often ask for psychological help than men (and in doing so influence statistical analyses); they also face frustrating barriers to career satisfaction that men do not. Still, these figures are impressive. To us, however, they are no surprise. For several years we have been in the business of helping people live to their greatest potential through our motivational speeches and Life Plus seminars. We define Life Plus as the ability to experience joy, happiness, success, good health, and loving relationships a majority of the time. However, many women have told us over and over that worry, anxiety, and negativity stand in the way of their success and that they feel helpless to do anything about it. Here is what they say is caused by common, everyday worry:

- Physical problems such as insomnia, headaches, backaches, ulcers, even anxiety and panic attacks.
- Relationship problems between men and women, mothers and children, family members, friends, and co-workers.
- Poor job performance, low productivity, and financial woes.
- Low self-esteem and depression, which cause women to function far below the level of their capabilites.

We believe that women don't have to fall into the worry trap. We have developed five easy-to-master "SKILL Tools" to help women break the habit of worry. We'll explain them in detail in later chapters, but first let's look at how worry got to be a female-shaped trap in the first place.

WHY WOMEN WORRY

In writing this book, we sought out the latest scientific studies and interviewed leading psychologists and psychiatrists on the subject of worry. We set up informal focus groups of women in all parts of the nation to tell us why they thought they worried. We also studied the thousands of letters we have received from women who read our previous books, *Anxiety and Panic Attacks*, *Beyond Fear*, and *The Life Plus Program for Getting Unstuck*, and who wanted our opinions about how they could solve their worry problems.

The four main paths that we have discovered lead women straight into the worry trap are described below.

THE PSYCHOSOCIAL PATH

From childhood on, most women are taught to defer to men in making decisions. As adults, they lack important problem-solving and decision-making skills. Because they have been trained since childhood to depend on Daddy and other males to make their decisions for them, they have difficulty taking charge when problems arise. Their only recourse, then, is to worry about, rather than to solve, their problems. When the problems only worsen, their self-esteem plummets. Feeling powerless to fix things, they worry more. It becomes a vicious cycle.

The growing numbers of successful, decisive women in business prove that this destructive heritage can be overcome. Our SKILL Tools can help you do the same.

THE INSTINCTIVE PATH

Whether women learn to nurture others or whether nurturing is instinctual, the fact is that most women are prone to worrying about other people's problems in addition to their own. Becoming a mother and taking responsibility for the complete well-being of a baby seems to strengthen this instinct. Many women transfer this desire to protect to other relationships as well. They "help" others by worrying about them.

THE SOCIETAL PATH

As women attempt to fulfill the many roles that today's society demands—wife, lover, mother, and financial provider—stress intensifies, and opportunities to worry increase. "Old-boy networks" may stand in the way of career advancement, while male attitudes let women know that "it isn't feminine" to be assertive. At the same time, some working women worry that lack of time with their families is causing them to be "bad mothers." Even women who don't work outside the home are under stress, because society approves of women who achieve in the workplace and discounts the importance of full-time homemaking and mothering.

THE PHYSIOLOGICAL PATH

It is possible that women's bodies "set them up" for worry. Hormonal fluctuations cause depression for millions of women affected by PMS, hysterectomies, postpartum problems or menopause. The sensitivity women sometimes feel as a result of hormonal fluctuations can increase their sense of a loss of control.

Moreover, scientists have found dissimilarities in the physiology of men's and women's brains that show that women actually perceive more to worry about. Studies by Christine de Lacoste-Utamsing of the University of Texas Health Science Center and Ralph Holloway of Columbia University, published in the June 25, 1982, issue of *Science*, reported that gender differences exist in the shape and surface area of the human corpus callosum, a large bundle of nerve fibers connecting the right and left hemispheres of the brain. This difference could mean that women have more nerve fibers connecting the two hemispheres than men; hence women's brains are less lateralized. In other words, women use both hemispheres for tasks for which men use only one. Some anthropologists interpret this data to mean that females have "wide-angle" vision while males have "tunnel" vision. For example, in their societal roles, women, usually responsible for protecting several children of various ages from danger, may have adapted by developing an ability to perceive many different stimuli at the same time. Men, the hunters, learned to avoid distractions because they themselves might have been killed had they not concentrated on their prey. While this physical difference gives women the advantage in understanding human relationships, it also means that they gather more data about which they can choose to worry, and they do.

WHY YOU DON'T HAVE TO WORRY

Do you have to walk down those four pathways leading straight to the female worry trap? We say no. Culture, cognitions, and female behavior *don't* have to converge in women to create anxiety that undermines health, self-esteem, and productivity.

The Psychosocial and the Instinctive Paths to Worry are actually learned behaviors. Even though many women have been taught since childhood to be dependent, they can learn problem-solving skills that will enable them to function powerfully in the world. And if they take on others' problems because they have become nurturers, they can learn how to let go when necessary.

While the Societal Path to Worry is real, women can choose to deal with stressors differently. Bob discovered this was true when he recovered from panic attacks and agoraphobia. A panic attack occurs when the body interprets an overwhelming amount of stress as danger and calls in a "fight or flight" response. When no visible sign of danger exists, it is terrifying to experience the pounding heart, dry mouth, nausea, and the feeling of faintness that go along with panic attacks. Agoraphobia, often defined as a fear of open places, is actually the fear of having a spontaneous panic attack. It develops when people try to *avoid* places where these frightening attacks occurred. Gripped by this most devastating of all phobias, Bob was housebound and suicidal. When, to his great relief, he learned that it was not the amount of stress he had in his life that caused anxiety but the way he handled it, he was able to turn his life around. He developed tools to *manage* stress and desensitize himself to his fear, without the aid of tranquilizers or other medications. Using these tools, he recovered completely. Since then he has taught tens of thousands of agoraphobics, the majority of whom have been women, that they can remain calm in the face of overwhelming stress, and he has given them tools with which they can lessen the effects of stress. We will share these tools with you later in this book.

For the Physiological Path to Worry scientists report that only a few women are seriously affected by hormone fluctuations. For those who are, doctors offer hormone replacement therapy which has benefitted from refinements in methods measuring the amounts and types of hormones needed and the ways of administering them to make them more effective. Studies show that carefully prescribed medication, along with diet, exercise, and mental conditioning, can help women affected by PMS, by the changes that occur during menopause, or those that occur after a hysterectomy.

As for women's having wide-angle vision, which allows them to perceive more worrisome data, we can show you how not to respond to this data with worrying. You can lessen anxiety by restructuring your thoughts, using our SKILL Tools, and relaxing your body through fitness and stretching exercises. You can also simply *decide* not to worry.

The Penn State study points out the role of gender identification: If women buy into the gender role, which is considered "feminine," they will worry more. "In our society considerable consensus exists regarding the nature of masculine and feminine roles," it reports. "Worry has been traditionally identified as a feminine, gender-role stereotypic trait by both males and females. Perhaps as women often endorse a feminine gender-role they are more likely to report worry."

Can women choose to endorse a different gender role identification and free themselves from worry? We like what Gloria Steinem told the *D Magazine* Women's Conference in Dallas on March 16, 1989. She drew parallels between the experience of women, seen as a minority group, and immigrant groups. Every immigrant group that has come to the United States has been labeled with stereotypical weaknesses that in the end have been proven false, she said.

"Gunnar Myrdal's *American Dilemma* makes us understand that the myths of inferiority that have always afflicted women of all races are parallel to those that afflicted black men and men from other discriminated-against groups . . . whether it was smaller brains, passive natures, childlike natures, the inability to govern ourselves, or special job skills. . . . The Smithsonian published a book titled *Apes, Angels and Irishmen*, which accumulated all the racial myths extant in science, universities, cartoons, and pop culture that definitively proved with skull measurements that the Irish were descended from the apes and the English from angels. Once you have read this stuff you will never feel the same about any biological argument," she said to a cheering audience. "We don't trouble ourselves with these myths."

BE HAPPY, DON'T WORRY?

Is it enough simply to tell yourself that the assumptions made about women are false? Can you just decide to stop worrying and become happy? In our Life Plus seminars we teach people how to be happy, but not by repressing their fears and worries. We explain how to harness both the conscious and unconscious mind through goal setting, new ways of thinking, visualization techniques, and other simple strategies to help people confront and solve problems. It is not about ignoring problems. We teach people how to *nurture themselves through* their problems.

To help women win out over worry, we have formulated five SKILL Tools which we will help you master in this book:

1. Seek the real reason for your worry.
2. Know your alternatives.
3. Image your goals.
4. Let yourself risk.
5. Let go of problems.

By learning to use the SKILL Tools, you can escape the worry trap. You can solve problems and make decisions rather than get stuck in anxiety and powerlessness. And you won't become "unfeminine" by doing so.

PEARL WORRY VERSUS THE WORRY-GO-ROUND

The women in our focus groups repeatedly told us what we already suspected: There are two kinds of worry, a "good" kind of worry that leads to constructive action, and a bad kind that undermines health, self-esteem, and productivity.

We call the good kind "pearl worry." When a grain of sand works its way into a tightly closed oyster shell, the oyster secretes a protective liquid to insulate against the irritation. After many such secretions, the oyster creates a pearl of great value and beauty. It not only overcomes the irritation, but produces an unexpected gift. When your worry leads you to take action and change your behavior, you may receive unexpected benefits in your life and in the lives of others that are of great value and beauty.

Being on the "worry-go-round" is the self-defeating type of worry that so many women tell us about. They climb aboard and spin dizzily around in circles, thinking they are doing something constructive to help themselves or prevent bad things from happening. When no change occurs, they become angry and depressed, but do they get off? No! Even though they are completely worn out, they hold on for dear life. Doing this will get you as far as running on a treadmill.

Almost all of the women in our focus groups admitted to being on the worry-go-round a large part of every day. Typical comments were "Worry makes me neurotic, bitchy, unable to sleep." "It makes me self-critical," "disorganized," "emotionally self-abusing," or "mentally and emotionally paralyzed." "It gives me headaches."

Few women in our focus groups did pearl worrying. When they did, they said, "Worry has been a positive force in my life because it led me to take action," or "It pushed me to look for solutions."

We ourselves have known both kinds of worry. Before learning how to pearl worry, Jane spent many a sleepless night on the worry-go-round imagining that her son was in trouble when he had not returned home on time. Bob kept telling himself, "I'm just a fraud," and felt inept in his job. Once we learned how to pearl worry, we discovered a greater gift than just a solution to a problem. We found a new way of living that was so wonderful we called it "Life Plus." To us, this meant a life that was filled with joy and happiness in spite of problems. That's what is possible for you: life without a worry-go-round, negativity, fear, or poor self-esteem.

We hope that you will want to master the five SKILL Tools. We will explain how we did that for ourselves in the next chapter.

CHAPTER 2

◆ ◆ ◆

What We Learned About the Psychosocial Path to Worry

Adele had a better-than-average job that offered no promise of advancement. She wanted to make a change but worried too much about making the break. She told us she felt "frozen."

"This is my biggest worry right now," she said. "What if I change jobs and don't make the right choice? What if I *don't* change jobs and end up without enough money? Whichever decision I make, I could suffer for it the rest of my life!" Then she shook her head, realizing she had given us the perfect description of being on the worry-go-round. Her mind was going in circles—but she was still in the same spot.

"I can get pretty creative with worry," she said ruefully. "I think it's because I watched my mother worry. Once when I was thirteen, Mother woke me at midnight. She was just frantic. She said, 'Adele, your sister went on that bike hike with her club all the way to the river today and she's not back yet.' I told her, 'Don't worry, Mom, she's probably with her friends at someone's house.' But Mom wouldn't listen. She had already visualized the worst.

" 'But Adele, she was wearing those tennis shoes!' By this time she was practically hysterical. 'What if her shoelace came untied and got tangled up in the spokes of her bike, and then what if she fell into the river and no one noticed? Oh, we'd better call the police!' "

Adele smiled, remembering. "Of course, my sister was at her friend's house, but somehow my mother's ability to create disastrous scenarios in her mind rubbed off on me. Now I do the very same thing. I imagine all sorts of things—both favorable and unfavorable—that other people are thinking. I can see and hear them talking to me and hear myself talking back. Sometimes the conversations become so real I think they really took place. At night before I go to sleep or in the morning when I wake up, my mind races in circles. My heart beats too fast. During the day I snap at people. I'm so preoccupied that I am unresponsive to what others are saying."

Adele learned to get on the worry-go-round by following the psychosocial path. Childhood circumstances, including the role model of a mother who worried compulsively, taught her to create catastrophes in her mind. Societal pressures to adopt a traditionally passive gender role reinforced the habit of worrying instead of taking action.

While many women in our focus groups reported that they had learned anxiety at their mother's knee, not all of them did. Even when parents displayed confidence and tried to instill self-esteem in their daughters, even when they raised their little girls to be as independent as their sons, still many of these women became worriers as adults because of a faulty self-perception that developed from other undercurrents or circumstances in their early years. In fact, many women found it impossible to identify the exact events in childhood that taught them how to imagine dire scenarios like Adele's.

"Worry is like a sport for which you don't need a racquet or clubs to play the game. You can do it whenever you want, whether you are by yourself or surrounded by people," said Jessica, a woman in our Florida focus group, who told us that her worry was like a bad habit that she couldn't seem to break, even though she wanted to.

We learned through our personal experience with worry that

the psychosocial path begins with real or imagined trauma. What actually happens, however, is not as important as your perception of what happens.

JANE'S EXPERIENCE WITH WORRY

When Jane was four years old, she pulled a pot full of scalding water from the stove and burned herself so badly that she almost died. During the weeks that she was hospitalized, most of her teeth deteriorated, decayed, and fell out prematurely. A nurse regularly shaved her head to cut down the chance of infection.

Jane was lucky to live through that ordeal, but when she returned home, she faced another. On her first trip to Sunday School, some of the children made fun of her ugly red scars, stubby hair, and toothless grin. Others were frightened of her. No one would play with her.

Her parents saw the hurt and rejection in Jane's eyes and realized that while the burns had healed, the scars were deep. They took their sad little girl home, gathered the family around, looked into Jane's eyes and told her, "What's beautiful about you is on the inside."

Every time a schoolmate made fun of her, her mother told her the same thing; her mother really tried to instill in Jane some self-esteem. Even so, Jane's perception of herself was still "Jane, the scarred one." To make matters worse, at nine years of age, she developed a form of bone cancer. She was lucky that the situation was detected early enough to be cured with massive doses of chemotherapy; but this second lengthy hospital stay caused her to think of herself as "Jane, the sick one."

"My perception of myself was not that I was not loved or that I was different because someone had abused me emotionally. Still, I definitely felt that I was not okay. I worried constantly about my appearance and whether I could get the love I thought I lacked," she said.

This poor self-esteem caused Jane to seek approval through overachievement. During high school, she entered a beauty pageant. Despite her scars she became Miss Winston-Salem, North Carolina. In college, she worried about being popular and won an election to become a class officer. When she was nineteen, some close friends got married and she panicked. "What if I get too old and no one wants to marry me?" she asked herself. So she got married.

When Jane had a baby, she got on the worry-go-round in earnest. "What if I don't do things right as a mother?" she thought. She was so anxious, she missed out on a lot of enjoyment with her son.

"One reason I took motherhood so seriously was that I kept asking myself, 'What would everyone think about *me* if *he* weren't perfect?' I wanted everyone to look at me and say, 'She did it right,' " Jane remembers.

She continued to overachieve by going back to college to get an M.A. while holding down two jobs and trying to be the perfect housewife and mother. True to her pattern, she also became a model teacher.

"On the outside, I looked like a winner, but all of my accomplishments came from the fact that inside I was telling myself, 'I know I'm not worthy, the way I am. I'm just Jane—the one with the scars.' So every time I did something good, a voice inside told me, 'Ha, you think that's good? It's not good enough. Do some more.' "

It was a vicious cycle. The more Jane worried about herself, the lower her self-esteem became. The less worthy she felt about herself, the more anxious she became. This pushed her to achieve more, and then she would discount her achievements and undermine herself all over again. For many years Jane felt so dependent on her mother's constant reassurances that she was okay that she developed an illogical fear that her mother, while quite healthy, was going to die. "I would hear a siren and rush to the telephone to see if Mother was okay," she said. She was having marital problems, too. Then came a move to Texas with many painful adjustments, and her marriage eventually ended in divorce. Forced to make some decisions for herself, she chose to enter therapy to overcome her lack of self-esteem. At last the inner critic was silenced.

"Not until I was forty did I realize that despite my scars, I was really okay," Jane says. With enhanced self-esteem, she could see a problem as a nudge to action rather than self-recrimination. She also realized that it was acceptable to do things for herself that she enjoyed. She pursued a career in public speaking, then formed an all-female corporation and began speaking to Fortune 500 corporations about human potential in the marketplace. A few months before she met Bob, she wrote down her criteria for the kind of man she wanted to marry. When she began dating Bob, she found that he fulfilled almost all her expectations. After they were married, they began teaching Life Plus workshops, helping both sexes become less prone to worry. She feels that she learned a lot— including the necessity to take the responsibility for her own happiness rather than being dependent on Bob or on her work to create it for her.

"It's been a long trek, and even now I catch myself in worry thoughts. When I begin thinking, 'What if?,' I don't start fretting, ruminating, and turning my insides out over a problem. I apply the five SKILL Tools that Bob and I have developed to teach others how to stop worrying. Then I can move from being concerned to taking action. Many times pearl worry brings me rewards I wouldn't have dreamed were possible."

When Jane started sharing her ideas on worry, women told her how they got on the worry-go-round too. She began to see the relationship between low self-esteem and the habit of worry.

"I have come to realize that my childhood was no more traumatic than that of most people. All of us have scars. Perhaps your parents died when you were a child or you continually did poorly in school. Maybe your parents were alcoholics or they even abused you. Or maybe nothing out of the ordinary happened to you. You don't have to have real scars to have low self-esteem. It's your perception of yourself that counts," Jane says. "And that perception can make all the difference in whether or not you worry."

WHAT AGORAPHOBIA TAUGHT BOB ABOUT WOMEN AND WORRY

Bob's story proves that psychological perceptions of your gender role have a lot to do with whether or not you are a worrier. Looking at his childhood, Bob sees that he took on the passive, dependent nature that psychologists identify as the female gender role. Perhaps it stemmed from the fact that he was born with a club foot. Although surgery eventually corrected the problem, he was left with a slightly withered leg—and a legacy of abuse from other boys. He felt inferior and insecure. He thought that he could not do the things that he wanted to do. This perception of himself eventually caused him to fulfill his expectations. In seven years after graduating from college, he held six different jobs in sales and sales management. He always looked good when he applied for the job, but his lack of-self esteem prevented him from producing.

Finally, when he created his own executive search firm, he became successful—at least on the outside. On the inside, however, worry, anxiety, and depression were his constant companions.

"An inner voice kept telling me that I was not a worthy person. If I accomplished something with my business, it wasn't as good as it should have been. I lived with the fear that I was going to be discovered for what I thought I was—a fraud," he says.

When Bob was thirty-three, his father died, and Bob spent a lot of time trying to comfort his mother. Bob couldn't handle this increased stress. His worry and anxiety built higher and higher. It was as if he had a rain barrel inside that contained his stress. Then one day, as he was reading the *Wall Street Journal* in his office, an activity that was not stress-producing at all, his worry spilled over the top of the rain barrel. Recognizing danger, his body instantly released adrenaline to enable him to fight or flee. The panic attack that resulted from this sudden overload of adrenaline felt to him like a heart attack, but his doctors could not identify the problem and prescribed only tranquilizers. The strange attacks repeated themselves and became more severe. Fearing that somehow the places where he had the panic attacks were causing them, Bob avoided returning to those places. The more he worried, the more attacks he had and the more places he told himself he couldn't go. Soon he was housebound with agoraphobia. If he tried to open the front door to pick up the morning paper, he had a panic attack. Then he had a new worry: Was he crazy? He was nearly suicidal before he discovered how to turn his life around.

In his first book, *Anxiety and Panic Attacks*, Bob tells how he overcame his agoraphobia without the use of medications. He started desensitizing himself to his panic by taking risks and going outside his home. He lessened his fear of leaving home by using visualizations and affirmations to gain the help of his unconscious mind. He practiced ways of thinking positively instead of negatively, he worked to increase his self-esteem, and he started setting and accomplishing goals. By the time he had recovered from agoraphobia, he had mastered tools for mental, physical, and spiritual improvement. He applied them to lose weight, become physically fit, and to launch a career in public speaking so that he could tell everyone that they too could experience this wonderful transformation that he called Life Plus. Bob has helped tens of thousands of people use these same recovery tools.

Through participation in the Phobia Society of America, Bob learned that some scientists have done research that seems to prove that agoraphobics are genetically predisposed to this type of anxiety. About 70 percent of reported agoraphobics are women. Why should females be afflicted much more often than men? Was there a physical difference? Through interviews with some of the leading therapists and doctors working with phobias, Bob learned that other experts believe that stress, rather than a genetic fault, causes agoraphobia. Christopher J. McCullough, Ph.D., author of *Managing Your Anxiety*, interpreted the data in the very same studies to show that "people who suffer anxiety attacks are simply normal people under prolonged stress. Their bodies are overproducing adrenaline (epinephrine) and, as a consequence, the muscles in their bodies continuously contract."

Bob's experience in working with agoraphobics taught him that those who are passive about their stress and take no action to prevent the concerns in their lives from turning into worry and anxiety are subject to panic attacks. If they don't nurture themselves and build their self-esteem, the panic attacks may become more frequent. By avoiding places where they have had the attacks, they become agoraphobic. This passive, dependent way of reacting to stress is what psychologists identify as the feminine gender role. Most women identify with it and that is why more women than men have panic attacks.

Bob says, "I believe that a lot of women and men who have a feminine gender identity develop the bad habit of worrying, and some of them become agoraphobic. But you don't have to have panic attacks, even if you should be genetically predisposed to them. You can get over the bad habit of worrying by setting goals and using some simple tools to cut back on the production of adrenaline in your body."

WHAT WORRIES WOMEN MOST?

When our focus groups reported what they worried about, it was easy to see that many had followed the Psychosocial Path to Worry. No matter what their childhood had been, they somehow developed low self-esteem, a poor perception of themselves, and a passive and dependent nature.

"Yes, we do worry, and we do it a lot," these women told us. With many women contributing to family income or assuming the role of primary breadwinner, *financial concerns* were the most common. "How will I get enough money to pay the bills?" they worry, or "What if I get sick and have no one to support my family?" or "I'll never have enough money to retire." Here are the other primary concerns:

- *Relationships.* "Finding someone who will love me," "losing my boyfriend or husband," "being alone"
- *Personal appearance.* "Being too fat," "too skinny," "having a bad complexion"
- *Pleasing (or not pleasing) others.* "How to be assertive without losing my femininity," "how to say no to requests without offending others"
- *Making the wrong decision.* "Questions about my career," "problems with my marriage," "whether or not to have a baby"
- *Health.* "What if I get a sexually transmitted disease?" "Who will take care of me if I develop a chronic illness?" "What if I never get over this minor illness I've got?"
- *Children's problems.* "Will I be a good enough mother?" "What if my children get involved with drugs?" "How can I protect

them from kidnappers and other dangers?" "Should I give
custody to my ex-husband?"

- *Not having enough time.* "Time for my job and my children,"
"everyone expects so much of me"
- *Growing old.* "Wrinkles," "Retirement funds" "What if I never
get married?" "What if I never have children?"
- *Job performance.* "What if I'm not doing a good enough job?"
"What if I am fired or laid off and can't find another job?"
- *Parents.* "Their health," "their expectations of me"
- *World affairs.* "Pcacc," "pollution," "morals," "drugs"

WHAT SCIENTISTS TELL US ABOUT WORRY

Perhaps in reading this list of worries you are wondering what the
difference is between a legitimate concern and worry. We are not
saying that it is wrong to feel fear about the consequences of
legitimate concerns, but it is harmful to let anxiety take over when
the fear is irrational. For instance, if your parents or children have
health problems, you will almost certainly be afraid for them. If
you don't have a job and the rent is due, it wouldn't be normal if
you were not anxious. But if you let your stomach be tied into
knots because you are afraid you will never meet the right man or
make the perfect report, your worry is irrational. According to Dr.
Kenneth Z. Altshuler, head of the psychiatry department at the
University of Texas Southwestern Medical School, "The difference between anxiety and fear is that fear has a legitimate object,
and anxiety doesn't. If you see a tiger and get frightened, that's
fear. If you don't see a tiger and you are frightened, that's
anxiety."

It is our conclusion that when you perceive yourself as being
unworthy, no tigers are around.

The Penn State study on worry reports, "The worrisome stim-
ulus can spring from within, as a fearful thought or image. Our
research indicates that the situations of most concern to the worrier
are social-evaluative in nature. Our experience and various findings
lead us to suggest that the underlying concern for the worrier is a
fear of failure or rejection. . . . We find that worriers *are preoccupied
with how they are perceived,* they review all potential situations, and

they become indecisive when a choice could mean potential failure or rejection." (Italics ours.)

This is a good description of worry-go-round thinking. We'll have more to say in the second part of this book about how to eliminate it from your life. Meanwhile, take a few minutes right now to answer the following questions. This quiz will help you see whether you are on the psychosocial path that leads to the worry-go-round. Read the statements and then check them as very false, mostly false, mostly true, or very true.

THE PSYCHOSOCIAL WORRY QUIZ

Statement	Very false	Mostly false	Mostly true	Very true
1. My mother was a worrier.				
2. My father/mother/other close relatives were worriers.				
3. My childhood was traumatic.				
4. I was emotionally, physically, or sexually abused as a child.				
5. I felt different from other children although I was fairly average.				
6. I felt different from other children because I really was different.				
7. I felt it was up to me to help my parents with financial or health problems.				
8. I failed in school both educationally and socially.				
9. I didn't fit in with the other kids in school because I always earned good grades.				
10. I never had a date while in high school.				

If you marked three or more of these statements as true or mostly true, you could easily have chosen the psychosocial path to the worry-go-round. At the same time, realize that scoring many "trues" and "mostly trues" does not automatically make you a worrier. After all, if you had brothers, they grew up with the same background you did. If they have avoided becoming worriers, it may be partly due to their male gender identification. They see themselves as able to find solutions to their problems. They are not so concerned with what other people think when they have a failure.

Inherited personality traits may also have a lot to do with whether or not you are a worrier. According to research published in the *Psychological Bulletin* by Southern Methodist University psychologists David Watson and Lee Anna Clark, the propensity to experience a negative emotional state is a personality trait that remains fairly consistent through the life of one who has it. "There is very strong evidence through studies in which identical twins were adopted into different families that being easily worried has a biological, genetic component. But biology isn't destiny. People can learn through self-regulation to involve themselves in activities that will change their moods. They can be more assertive about problem solving or distracting themselves from their worries," said Dr. Clark, who points out that people can experience *both* negative and positive moods simultaneously (such as when enjoying a scary movie) or they may be simply in a neutral mood. Some activities may make negative moods less intense while others may heighten a positive mood. For example, social activity affects only the positive moods whereas listening to music and relaxing lightens negative moods, but may or may not increase positive feelings.

Running, which is Dr. Clark's preferred form of exercise, tends to affect both kinds of moods. It lessens negativity and enhances a positive mood.

"There are days when I am feeling kind of blah and I don't really want to run, but I have learned from experience that if I force myself to run, I will feel better. That's the kind of thing that a person who may be naturally a worrier or low in the positive emotions can learn to do. They can force themselves to do things that they might not naturally do, knowing that the ultimate benefit might be positive," she said.

MAKE A PROMISE TO YOURSELF

If you want to get off the worry-go-round, the message is clear. Take action! The first thing you can do is to buy a loose-leaf notebook with ten dividers. On the first page, write out your goals:

1. I set my goal to get off the worry-go-round for _____.
2. I will read this book through two times.
3. Using the SKILL Tools, I will set up a plan to stop worrying.
4. I will follow my plan.

Mark another section "Why I worry." Write what you learned about which of the psychosocial paths you follow to worry. Write out some of the worrisome experiences that occurred during your childhood. If you perceived yourself as helpless, passive, or dependent, record those feelings. End with this statement: I have a choice about whether to worry or not.

Next, go on to chapter 3 and learn how the Instinctive Path leads to worry.

CHAPTER 3

◆ ◆ ◆

The Instinctive Path to Worry

We have a cousin who is a chronic worrier who told us, "All the years I was raising my daughter, I worried about her safety. Every time she walked to school or rode her bicycle or went on a date with a teenage driver, I was in turmoil. Then one Saturday my husband and I were completely relaxed enjoying our favorite music when my daughter said she was going to drive to the neighborhood store to buy some soft drinks. I didn't think anything about it—until the phone rang. It was the hospital telling me that our daughter had had an accident three blocks from our house and had a broken leg. *I couldn't believe that that had happened when I hadn't even worried about it,*" she said.

What about the hundreds of times that this woman had worried over her daughter and nothing happened? She suffered the very same anxiety she felt when the wreck actually occurred. She had developed migraine headaches trying to prevent accidents over which she had no control. How much better would it have been to learn techniques for releasing worry over situations in which she was powerless.

The mother of an eleven-year-old told us, "I worry about what's going to happen to Darlene. Soon she'll be a teenager. What if she gets in with the wrong crowd at school? What if she starts using drugs? Gets pregnant? Drops out of school?" This mother truly believes that *her fantasies are a way of protecting Darlene's well-being*. She does not realize that if she constantly pictures the worst, her daughter may fulfill her expectations. At the very least, she will worry herself sick for no reason.

Barbara, a divorced mother of two, told us that she worried for six months that her boyfriend was cheating on her. "I tried to find out in every way except the obvious one—confronting my fears and discussing them with him. 'Better the worry you know than the worry you don't know,' I told myself. I felt afraid to risk talking to him and somehow guilty about criticizing him, so I pretended that everything was okay, while I lay awake every night sick with worry. At the same time, a little thought in the back of my head kept saying, 'I know he's cheating and I'm willing to put up with it, because I'm a weak person.' As it turned out, all my worry did no good, because finally I discovered that he *was* cheating. I had put myself down for six months because I didn't treat either one of us like adults," she said.

These women followed what we call the Instinctive Path to Worry. They transformed the nurturing concern that is a normal part of being a mother into dysfunctional thinking and behavior.

Let's look at how this happens: Just as all female animals have instincts to protect their young, human mothers don't have to learn to be concerned for their babies' safety, health, and emotional well-being. Nature provides them with a fierce determination to protect and nurture, sometimes even at the cost of their own lives. Animals have the same instincts, but don't intellectualize their concern and turn it into worry; they simply take action to protect their young and go on their way. Human mothers are also aware of what others think and expect of them. When women are afraid that they can't measure up to accepted standards of mothering, they may fall into the worry trap.

FEMALE AND MALE INSTINCTS
ARE DIFFERENT

A woman learns nurturing behavior by following the role model provided by her mother and other women in her life. Society then rewards women for developing and following their nurturing instincts. If you're not convinced, go to a rack of Mother's Day cards and see how often the sentiment is, "You are a great mother because you take care of me." Whether you were born with this instinct or learned it doesn't really matter. You have it, society reinforces it, and it affects the way you relate to others. If you don't learn constructive ways to handle this instinct, you may, like the women mentioned above, find it leading you down the path to "Camp Run-Amok."

We're not saying that men don't have nurturing instincts—they do. But women are surrounded with cues to develop this instinct to its highest degree. Since prehistoric times, men have usually been the hunters while women were the nest-makers. The survival of the human race depended on how well women protected and nurtured their young. Furthermore, the parenting process for women is directly physical; for men, it exists outside themselves. For nine months the baby is a part of the woman's body. After birth, she may choose the satisfying experience of nursing her baby, while the most a man can do is hold a bottle, change a diaper, or walk the floor. Many women are so involved with their babies for several months after birth, and so affected by hormonal changes, that they may have decreased desire for intimate relations with a man. The infant that the mother sees as an emotionally satisfying extension of herself may appear as something of a rival to even the most loving father. A man may have the instinct to provide for and protect his child, but he can hardly feel the visceral connection women experience in carrying, birthing, and nurturing a baby.

Since society continues to reinforce the idea that the nurturing role is female, it often imposes guilt if a woman falls below the maternal standards set by others. Virtually no one asks a father whether he has put his baby into day care, but nearly everyone asks working mothers, "Who is taking care of your baby? Aren't you afraid he won't get proper care?" When a child becomes sick at school, the nurse calls the mother, not the father. When a child gets into trouble, the principal usually calls the mother. Little wonder that many women begin to worry, "Am I a good enough mother?" When guilt takes over, the nurturing instinct becomes a pathway to the worry-go-round. Men don't fall into this trap as readily because no one expects them to.

In her book, *Unfinished Business*, Maggie Scarf cited studies showing that for every male diagnosed as suffering from depression, the head count for females was anywhere from *two to six times* greater. Women became depressed for many reasons, but such lopsided statistics led Scarf to consider studies of the psychological effect of the materials that men and women read. In popular magazines for the male market, the content of both fiction and essays tended to address adventure, the overcoming of obstacles, triumph, and mastery. In the material written for women, the preoccupation was with how to relate to others emotionally, how to please others, and how to deal with loss—mainly, the disruption of crucial emotional bonds. In her interviews with depressed women, Scarf also found that some universal female problems concerned the need to be cared for and the need to care for and to nurture others. Clearly, depressed women have gotten the message that they are responsible for nurturing others, and they worry when they aren't able to do so.

For instance, midlife used to be the time when women took up knitting or bridge while they enjoyed the grandchildren at a distance. Now many have moved into the workforce or returned to college to develop new and fulfilling lives. Growing numbers, however, find themselves caught in the middle, caring for an elderly parent and a grandchild.

"I feel torn all the time," admits one of our middle-aged friends. "I find myself wondering, 'When is it going to be my turn?' "

Ironically, we see women who do a wonderful job of nurturing others but do not nurture themselves. This erodes self-esteem and sets the stage for a ride on the worry-go-round.

THE FACTOR OF CONTROL

Many women tell us they can't stop worrying over others because they feel that it is their *duty* to worry. Keeping in mind all the threats that life poses, they told us, is a way for them to maintain control over danger and stay alert to combat it.

Jane says, "When I worried about my son, Miles, it was because I didn't feel that I had any control. I would ask myself, 'Where is he? What's going on? Why hasn't he called? Did he do what he was supposed to do?' I had an incredible capacity to create catastrophes!

"People would tell me that I needed to let go, for my own sake as well as for his. But like plenty of other women, I didn't want to hear that letting go was good for me. 'I'm thinking about the well-being of my child; it doesn't matter what happens to me,' I would tell myself. 'He is more important than I am, and the only thing I can do to protect him is to worry.' "

How do women become convinced that worry helps them be in control? As we have pointed out, they learn from their mothers and grandmothers that worrying is a natural part of the mothering instinct. When we asked one of our focus groups if their mothers had been the worrying type, a Jewish friend of ours who agonizes about her children, her co-workers, and almost every person she meets responded, "Are you kidding? Mother is Jewish, and that means she is a world-class adrenalinholic who goes around wringing her hands and managing our lives. She lets you know that worrying is what you are supposed to do if you are a woman."

While countless comedians, writers, and ordinary sons and daughters have made jokes about the capacity of their Jewish mothers to worry, we learned that plenty of other ethnic groups have the same problem. A young Anglo-Protestant told us that her grandmother had complained, "You're not worrying enough about your baby. Mothers are supposed to worry."

A thirty-year-old of Mediterranean heritage told us that when she is riding in the car with her mother and the mother must stop the car suddenly, her mother still takes one hand off the wheel and lays it on her daughter's chest to keep her from falling forward!

While these seem like ridiculous and fairly innocent examples of the worry trap, they can have an insidious fall-out. As mothers model the Instinctual Path to Worry, they teach their daughters that they are powerless to solve problems and make decisions for themselves and those they love. Instead they encourage their daughters to climb aboard the worry-go-round and take the responsibility for problems that belong to loved ones. This can be the beginning of a codependent relationship in which the worrier frees others from taking the responsibility for consequences of their actions. Ultimately she makes herself miserable and encourages others to self-destruct.

THE CROSSROADS WITH CODEPENDENCY

Whether or not you are a mother, you may have learned to feel guilty if you *don't* take responsibility for the actions of husbands, parents, siblings, friends, and even bosses. If your parents lacked a sense of self-worth and self-acceptance and used you and your siblings to gain a sense of power, adequacy, and security, you grew up in a *dysfunctional family*. As a result you may believe that you are nurturing others when in reality you are depending on them for your identity.

"When I got married and moved to a different city, I was so worried about whether my parents could make it without me that I had nightmares and screamed in my sleep," said Beth. "It wasn't that they were sick or starving. I just had an overpowering feeling that they needed me. Even worse, I felt guilty because I wasn't helping them. It took me several years to discover that my parents did not need me nearly as much as I needed to *feel* that they needed me."

Beth's habit of worrying about her parents began when she was seven. That was the year she begged her mother to get a divorce because of her father's drinking. Instead, the troubled parents stayed together and Beth developed into the "hero child"—the one who overachieved in order to care for the family. Beth became the "assistant mother" who helped protect her younger sisters from her father's angry outbursts. She won all kinds of awards at school and preserved the family reputation. Although Beth took on more than her share of responsibility as a child, she got a lot of approval for what she was doing. Worrying about others seemed to have its rewards. When she moved away at last, her parents were left to their own resources. Beth couldn't believe they could make it without her. They needed her, she told herself. In reality, she needed the good feelings about herself that she always felt for taking over their responsibility.

Beth didn't have to be a mother to worry about the safety and well-being of others. She acquired the worry habit as a child when she learned survival behaviors in reaction to her dysfunctional family. In effect, she became *codependent*, because she lived in reaction to a primary stressor, her father. In our focus groups and among the women whom Bob has helped overcome agoraphobia, we found thousands who knew that they were putting up with abusive mates, rescuing their parents and children, and sacrificing themselves for unappreciative friends and bosses. They worried about what would happen to these important others if they didn't nurture them, solve their problems, and rescue them when they failed.

"Codependence is the most common family illness because it is what happens to anyone in any kind of a dysfunctional family," says the renowned counselor John Bradshaw in his illuminating book *Bradshaw On: The Family*. He explains that every dysfunctional family has a primary stressor, which could be either parent's alcoholism, sexual abuse, death, divorce, sickness or hypochondria, or moral or religious righteousness, among other traumatic situations. Members of the family experience the primary stressor as a threat and respond by becoming hypervigilant. In other words, nature provides for their bodies to be ready to fight or flee from the primary stressor at any moment by keeping their stores of adrenaline at a high level. When children from dysfunctional families become adults, they retain this hypervigilant worry state. Many of them are so anxious they develop panic attacks. Others simply worry and take over too much responsibility for their mates, children, lovers, friends, or almost anyone who becomes important in their lives. They may see this worry as a way of loving or caring for another person, not as a physical and mental state of hypervigilance.

Our friend Anne Sadosky, a professional speaker, demonstrates with a drawing of a radio dial how all kinds of personalities can be perceived as pleasant or unpleasant. She represents each type of personality, whether it is outgoing, introverted, calm, or vivacious, as a different "station." "Regardless of which station is tuned in, the music can be pleasant if it is not too loud," she says. "But when you turn the volume up, watch out! All those endearing traits of personality, when they crash on the eardrum, become jarring."

In our stress workshops, we like to use a similar visual to show how the nurturing instinct can turn into codependency. We draw a Worry Meter which registers the volume of your concern for others. At 40 decibels, your concern about others may be perceived by them as being pleasant. But when you turn up the volume to 140 decibels by constantly picturing the worst, by giving unwanted advice, by pushing and rescuing and sacrificing yourself, you create such an ear-splitting din that others only want to escape. Of course these others have a choice as to how they will react, but if they too come from a dysfunctional family, they may escape into alcohol, drugs, battering, or simply acting in an angry, hostile way.

Jim Wilson, of the Phobia Centers of the Southwest, the psychotherapist who helped Bob recover from agoraphobia, says that a catch-22 rule of nature applies to worry. "Whenever someone discovers something that doesn't make them feel better, they tend to do it *louder*. That is just human behavior. If somebody finds that worry doesn't make them feel better, they will do it all the more." Once your nurturing instinct has forked into the codependency crossroad, you may continue to make the same mistakes without knowing it.

We have a dear friend who goes on relating codependently with her entire family even though her children are all grown. Divorced, she could be enjoying the freedom she now has to develop her individual gifts and talents. Instead she is caring for a teenage niece because her sister can't cope with life. Her son and daughter, both divorced, are moving back into her home with their children. She worries mightily about them all. Meanwhile, she works harder than she should to help everyone financially. The volume on her worry meter is so loud that she has totally lost herself, and her family reacts by letting her do just that.

Jane says, "Being codependent means, 'I need you to need me.'" At best your codependency prevents others from taking the risks and responsibilities they must take in order to become self-actualized. At worst it encourages others to become addicted to harmful behavior through their expectations that you will bail them out."

THE EFFECT ON YOU

When your nurturing instincts escalate in this way, you not only hurt others, you hurt yourself. As you picture others in dangerous, unhealthy situations, *your* body is the one that becomes unhealthy with backaches, headaches, stomach upsets, or worse. When you stifle resentments because you feel that you "should" sacrifice yourself for another, you are the one who becomes depressed.

"Because the high school my teenagers attend has a big problem with marijuana and cocaine, I've joined a mothers' group that fights drugs," says Laura. "We ask parents to monitor their kids' parties to keep out drug users. We bring in experts to speak at our meetings. We read everything we can to become informed about drugs. Certainly I'm concerned, but I can deal with the problem."

Jan, whose teenagers attend the same school, says, "I'm scared stiff that my kids will start taking drugs. I can't sleep because I imagine all kinds of terrible things happening to them. When they're away and the telephone rings, I just know they've been arrested, or been in a bad auto accident, or even that they're dead. I'm a nervous wreck."

There is often a difference between our *perception* of the truth and the actual facts. On a cloudy day, everything seems dark, but the sun is still there, shining above the thunderheads. If you have let your nurturing instincts turn into codependency, you are focusing too much on the clouds. The first step to receiving the love, light, and healing that is there for you is to decide whether you are on that Instinctual Path to Worry.

The following self-assessment will help you perceive the truth about yourself. Answer the questions true or false:

THE INSTINCTUAL WORRY QUIZ

	True	False

1. A good mother ought to worry about her children so that they will feel loved.

2. When my co-workers make mistakes, I feel that it is up to me to help them overcome the consequences.

3. When friends/parents/mates make important decisions, I get irritated if they don't consult me.

4. When friends/parents/mates make important decisions, I often tell them the better way to do things.

5. When my children get in trouble at school, it is a reflection on me as a mother.

6. I feel that it is up to me to protect my teenagers from taking any risk that might harm them.

7. If I don't visit my parents at least once every two weeks I feel guilty.

8. If others see me worrying about them, they will not do things that are destructive to them.

9. If I just try hard enough, I can change the destructive way my husband/lover/children live.

10. I help a lot of other people, but they never seem to help me in return.

11. Sometimes I feel like a failure as a mother.

12. When my boss or a colleague makes a mistake, I am quick to take the blame.

If your answer to more than half these questions is yes, you tend to take the Instinctual Path to Worry. After recording your answers in your journal, write down some of the incidents in your childhood that might have changed your nurturing instincts into a twenty-four-hour-a-day ride on the worry-go-round. For instance, did you as the oldest child feel responsible for protecting the younger children from your parents' anger/addiction/irresponsibility? Did your parents discipline you by shaming you

with the results of your actions so that you now feel that everything that goes wrong is your fault? This information will be
helpful when you work on the tools for letting go that we will
explain in later chapters.

CHAPTER 4

♦ ◆ ♦

The Societal Path to Worry

In 1978, a female college graduate could expect to be paid at the same level as a male high school drop-out, according to a study by J. L. Laws published in *Psychological Dimensions*. By 1989, 2 percent of corporation officers were female. This advancement did not come without sacrifice on the part of the women who won those lofty positions. A dynamic woman in her mid-thirties who became a partner in a prestigious Wall Street firm told us off the record that she had had to work much harder than the men with whom she competed.

"My timing was right. I was in the influx of the first women who attended Harvard Business School and the first group of young women to be accepted on Wall Street for entry level positions with the possibility of making partner. But some of my luck was self-generated. Young male associates worked 100 hours a week and traveled three days. I worked 115 hours a week and traveled four days," she told us. "Then I did something women are often loath to do—I took a risk. I moved three times in five years, opening new offices for the firm. I took on the toughest responsibility, which is generating new business."

This woman felt that she would not have been promoted if she had had children.

"Women in the business world are really in hostile territory in many ways. We need organized mentoring programs and seminars where we can learn the rules. Corporations must work to have open access for promotions for women and to break down the 'old boy' networks," she said.

Until corporations offer these amenities, many women will follow what we call the Societal Path to Worry. Fired with expectations but unable to deal with the real barriers which the workplace imposes on women, they jump onto the worry-go-round. Some meet stressful situations head-on; others stew. "What if I'm not doing the right thing?" they ask themselves. "What will people think of me if I become more assertive?" "What will they think of me if I don't?" "How can I do all the things I am expected to do?"

The social upheaval since the late sixties has affected much more than women's career opportunities, and it has caused anxiety for both men and women. Housing, medical, and educational costs soared while salaries stagnated. By 1989, 57 percent of families in the United States had husband and wife both working to make ends meet. According to pollster Louis Harris, baby boomers worked five and a half more hours a week in 1988 than they did fifteen years before, causing a loss of nearly ten hours of weekly leisure time. A survey published in the *Journal of the American Medical Association* suggests that as many as one of every four baby boomers has had a bout with chronic-fatigue syndrome.

In many ways, women have borne more of the burden of the changes. According to a poll for *Time* magazine and CNN by Yankelovich Clancy Shulman in 1989, 73 percent of the women compared to 51 percent of the men in two-income families complained of having too little leisure time. Women suffered the same career anxieties as men, but women alone found promotions blocked by the "glass ceiling." (They were close enough to the top echelons of business to be noticed, but discrimination prevented their becoming executive officers themselves.) In addition, they were still the primary care givers. They faced the physical stress of carpools, taking parents and children to the doctor, cooking the meals, and cleaning house. They also had to deal emotionally with issues that affected their children—inadequate day care, the dangers of drug abuse, and increasing crime. On top of all this, they were supposed to look slim, sexy, and beautiful and excel at work—all at the same time.

Single mothers (half of all marriages end in divorce), face even more societal stress. A one-paycheck family can be a ticket to poverty. Child rearing is harder. When single parents remarry, they often have the stress of learning to relate to stepchildren.

When management expert Felice Schwartz proposed the "Mommy Track" in 1989 as a career solution for women who wanted to give priority to home and family, we believe that she may have increased stress for some working women. Feminists said that corporations might require women to decide in their early twenties whether they wanted to give priority to their careers or to having children. Furthermore, it was theorized that the Mommy Track could provide corporations with a new excuse for not promoting women.

WORRIES ON THE SOCIETAL PATH

When we asked the women in our focus groups whether the changing role of women caused them to worry, those with children replied yes more frequently than those without.

"The changing role is just one more stress. I have more obligations to my family, job, and friends. Because I have greater aspirations for success, I also have more fear of failure," said a thirty-eight-year-old executive secretary.

"I thought I could take care of myself, so I divorced. Now I worry about finances. There is never enough money and there never will be as long as I'm alone," said a forty-seven-year-old office worker.

Many upwardly mobile single women in our focus groups told us that they approved of the changes. "I'd rather worry because I have a lot of options that women didn't use to have than be trapped in a life without them," said one. Still, women's lack of preparation to deal with societal change was evident in what most women listed as their chief worries:

WOMEN'S FIVE TOP WORRIES

1. *Money*. Not having enough money and being limited by sexist attitudes in their efforts to earn more.
2. *Looks*. The burden of maintaining standards of beauty as a way of controlling their destinies.
3. *Health*. The concern over sexually transmitted diseases (STDs) and lack of money and other resources needed to stay fit.
4. *Children*. Having to take the burden of responsibility for child care and fearing that the children would feel unloved because they were too busy to mother them "properly."
5. *Relationships*. Finding someone to love when men's and women's expectations have changed.

WHY YOU DON'T HAVE TO TAKE THE SOCIETAL PATH TO WORRY

Why do women take on these kinds of worries? Again, we see societal influences in childhood as the culprit. First of all, most female children were not raised to solve problems and make decisions. Daddy did it for them. Now that gender roles have changed, women are having to take responsibility for meeting their own needs without having the skills to do so. That puts tremendous pressure on them.

Furthermore, most little girls learn to equate love with how pretty, cute, good, and sweet they are, because parents compliment them for having those qualities. Trained to become pleasers of others and negators of their own needs, women lack self-esteem and show it in the worry questions, "Did I do it right?" and "Why can't I be good enough?"

Just because you were raised to be a pleaser doesn't mean that you have to stay that way. Our SKILL Tools will help you develop decision-making abilities along with a sense of self-worth. For now, let's take a look at the most common worries on the societal path and note how the lack of decision-making skills worsens them.

MONEY WORRIES

The women in our focus groups put money worries at the top of their list. Would they ever have enough of it to live as they wanted? What would happen if they got sick and couldn't work? How would they earn enough for a secure retirement? As societal roles have changed, women have taken on all the worries about finances that men shouldered in the past. These are real concerns, but we feel that women can best deal with them by learning how to set priorities, make decisions, and take risks rather than by giving in to anxiety and negative thinking.

Others worried about their inability to advance in their careers. "it seems that I ought to be able to achieve more, but I always get sidetracked by a man," said one. Women who attempt to achieve in business, education, religion, and government find these institutions controlled by men. The workplace becomes a source of frustration rather than reward, as evidenced by *Glamour* magazine's "Happiness Report" (April, 1989), in which 1,155 male and female respondents were questioned about the sexual revolution and the women's movement. It showed that for men, self-esteem rises along with income. Women earning over $35,000, however, reported *lower* self-esteem than those who made *less money!* Female respondents explained that more stress on the job invaded their romantic relationships, and also gave them more responsibility without the authority to go with it. Some felt they would be trapped at middle-management levels.

As a result of this glass ceiling, more women started new businesses in 1988 than did men, but many female entrepreneurs have discovered that being their own boss didn't spare them from worrying about finances.

"Money and financial security are my top worries," said a woman in one of our focus groups who made $130,000 in her own business in 1988. "I try to anticipate problems and prepare for them by worrying. It makes me feel like I'm in control of all those things for which I am responsible. Furthermore, with the changing role of women, I worry about how I should dress and how assertive I should be. Should I be "feminine" and weak? Is it okay to be seen as a good business manager?"

This talented and successful businesswoman suffered back pain and nightmares because she worried about what other people would think of her assertiveness!

We can't change the skew of the workplace, but we can offer problem-solving skills and ways to achieve assertiveness that will help you deal with male bias and decrease anxiety about your role in life.

WORRIES ABOUT YOUR APPEARANCE

When Jane was a little girl, forty-five-year-old women looked and acted almost elderly. They put their hair in buns, and wore clunky shoes and sexless blue/black dresses. Today, Joan Collins, Jane Fonda, and Linda Evans have set examples of midlife glamour. Woe be unto you if you discover cellulite at any age! Diet clinics and fitness centers are on every corner. Women spend millions on cosmetics and plastic surgery to eliminate crow's feet, facial blemishes, and wrinkles.

When Jane recently made a speech to a civic organization in a city of 150,000, she was seated at a table with eight members of the Junior League. These women, who held volunteer positions of great responsibility, said nothing about social issues. Instead, they talked about how much weight each had lost or gained, hairstyles, and clothes. "Occasionally someone would worry over a teenager or money, but appearance was the big thing," said Jane.

If you, like these intelligent women, worry about your looks, you may have been taught as a little girl that looking pretty is the way to attract a Prince Charming who will take on all your responsibilities and solve your problems for you. Despite the fact that today you may be the controller of a corporation or a successful entrepreneur, the myth remains that at home you are supposed to be unruffled, womanly, and feminine. On the job, you must look attractive (but of course, not *too* attractive) to men, or you'll never progress.

We don't think there is anything wrong with looking beautiful. Jane jokes that if legislators were considering outlawing the use of cosmetics, she would make a run on her local drug store and buy out the whole cosmetics department so that she would never lack for beauty supplies! We do believe that something is wrong, however, with being so obsessed about your appearance that you reproach yourself for your looks and the natural process of maturing. With increased self-esteem, you will feel more beautiful and consequently look that way too.

WORRIES ABOUT HEALTH

The women in our focus groups worried a lot about health. "Even when I'm not sick, I'm afraid that I'm going to get sick," said one. "And when I really am sick, even it it's just a minor illness, I'm afraid I will never get well." Part of this worry, we feel, is because women are expected to fulfill so many roles. They literally can't afford to get sick! Yet persistent worry gives them the headaches, stomach upsets, and back pains that make them fear they might have a serious illness. It's a vicious cycle which many women could break by taking action to help themselves become fit.

One big health worry is the possibility of being exposed to AIDS. "I don't know how to talk to men about AIDS, so I worry a lot," said one sexually active single woman. This is a genuine concern which we hope she will learn to address. It is imperative for all women to become assertive enough to discuss AIDS risks with their sexual partners.

WORRIES ABOUT CHILDREN

A recent study by *Parenting* magazine reported that while 74 percent of fathers acknowledged they should share child-care chores with the mother, only 13 percent actually fulfilled their duty. The demands of a career and the resulting loss of time that women can give their children increase the chances that nurturing instincts will evolve into worry. "I'm so tired after working on the job all day, and in the house all evening, that I can't read my preschooler a story before he goes to bed. I just want to get him to sleep so that I can collapse," said one young mother. Another said she worried about the effect she was having on her children when she picked them up from the day-care center. Fatigue made her so irritable that she felt she was making an indelibly bad impression on them.

Another big worry, worse for women than men, is what to do with children when they are ill. "Should I use some of my limited sick time to stay home with my child? Or should I send him to the day-care center with a cold and hope it doesn't get worse? What if I don't take my daughter to the doctor and then learn too late that her stomachache is really appendicitis?" said one woman.

When children become teenagers and begin to assert themselves as individuals, it sometimes seems as if parental control vanishes. Since women are still the acknowledged care givers, they feel the resulting anxiety more than most men. At around the same time, many women also have to start caring for ailing parents. Their concerns multiply, and there isn't enough time to accomplish what they feel they must.

We saw a recent commercial for a hospital that treats addicts and other troubled people, which made us realize how society feeds women's guilt over being less than perfect mothers. It showed a woman pacing the floor and wringing her hands. "It's 3 A.M. and my son hasn't come home. And I don't even know how to begin to tell my husband what the principal told me he did today at school," she said.

"Why can't she tell her husband? He's *his* son, too, isn't he?" Jane argues. "But she is assuming total responsibility. Women want to please so badly and want everything to be perfect, and feel at fault if it's not."

Women can't fight the instinct to nurture, nor should they. Nor can we change immediately the inequalities in child-rearing responsibilities for working women. We believe, however, that learning to use our SKILL Tools to make decisions will help women deal with problems with their children. By developing a sense of self-worth, they can give up the guilt they feel for being less than the perfect wife/professional.

RELATIONSHIP WORRIES

"Finding someone to love" remains a top priority for women today, but a changing society makes that quest all the harder. Gone are the days when women could live happily ever after by getting married and turning their problems over to a husband. For a man, the days are past when his wife spent all her time supporting his needs. Although both sexes retain fantasies of this idyllic life, the reality is two-career families, shared responsibilities, pressures of long-distance marriages, and tension about whose career is more important.

"Many men don't want to get married. If they do, they expect you to carry your financial weight—and women's salaries haven't caught up with men's. In the past men expected their wives to be mothers and lovers. But men don't take care of women anymore. Even worse, we don't have any role models to show us how to relate to men in this way," said one.

Some women hold on to their careers and marriages, but worry about whether they are still feminine or whether their relationships with their husbands suffer. Others follow the tradition of being subservient to a husband who functions as the head of the house. When the husband acts irresponsibly, his wife must battle her resentments.

Among over-thirty women in our focus groups, we sensed desperation among those who were single, divorced, or without significant others. "What's wrong with me? Why haven't I found someone?" were typical worry questions. Others wanted someone but were critical of men's attitudes. "I want to share the rest of my life with someone who will love me—but who will also care about what I think and support my accomplishments," said another. "How will I ever find that when men are so wrapped up in thinking about themselves?"

Married women frequently worried that they would lose the relationship because of the pressures of two-career marriages. Lack of communication, responsibilities for children, and disagreements over finances were sore points. Many women admitted they were just too tired to nurture the relationship. In addition, television talk shows discussing affairs and infidelity sometimes fanned suspicions about how husbands related to other women at work.

Divorced women without children worried that the scars of their first marriage would ruin their chances for happiness in a second liaison. Divorced women with children had the same worries plus the stress of dealing with custody and visitation issues. They also worried about finding men willing to love them *and* their children.

To deal with these concerns caused by a changing society, we believe women need to increase their sense of competence and self-worth. One woman expressed this need when she told us, "I've always thought of myself as a frog rather than a princess." Women certainly shouldn't think of themselves as frogs, but picturing themselves as princesses only means problem solving by finding Prince Charming and no change in their present mind-set. When women learn assertiveness and problem-solving skills, they reap the reward of self-worth, and both men and women worry less.

DON'T FORGET THE PLUSSES, TOO!

Jane had lived in North Carolina all her life until she moved to Texas in 1982. She had always worked as a schoolteacher. The move made her realize that she wanted to get out of the womb of the classroom, which was ruled by male principals and school administrators.

"When I made the change, I saw incredible opportunities. I explored the job market and ended up with a public-speaking career because I enjoyed the freedom it gave me. As recently as a decade ago, I, as a woman, wouldn't have been able to make this career change, because major corporations didn't invite women to speak to their employees about increasing their human potential," Jane points out.

Women in our focus groups told us that their worries about their changing roles were influenced by how they were trained as little girls. All had concerns about a changing society, but those who were taught to problem-solve as children, or who had learned it later in life, felt confident enough to benefit from those changes. We want you to reap some of the plusses too.

ARE YOU ON THE SOCIETAL PATH
TO WORRY?

To discover whether you are succumbing to societal pressures by becoming stuck in worry, mark the statements below as very true, sometimes true, or rarely true:

THE SOCIETAL WORRY QUIZ

	Very true	Sometimes true	Rarely true

1. I frequently apologize for the fact that I work by explaining that my husband and I need two paychecks.

2. I will never be able to make as much money as I need because women never get promoted in my company.

3. I feel that men look down on women who are sharp business people.

4. I am not satisfied with the career opportunities presented to me.

5. I worry about how to dress appropriately on the job.

6. I am too fat/skinny/wrinkled/facially blemished/etc.

7. I spend too much money on my appearance, but I feel it is a necessity.

8. When I have a headache or a backache that won't go away, I worry that I am developing symptoms of a serious illness.

9. I don't know how to talk about sexually transmitted disease to men in whom I might be sexually interested.

10. Since my mother developed ulcers at an early age, I am likely to do the same.

11. I feel guilty when I can't go to PTA meetings because I'm working.

12. I feel guilty because I don't work and I can't give my children the advantages I would like to give them.

13. When my child fails in school, it is my fault.

The Societal Worry Quiz *(continued)*

	Very true	Sometimes true	Rarely true

14. When my children are ill, I imagine that they are coming down with a life-threatening illness.

15. When my teenagers get into trouble, I prefer to cover it up rather than talk about solutions with my husband and with them.

16. It is my responsibility to make our home a relaxing place for my husband and children.

17. When my boyfriend/husband is feeling blue, it is my responsibility to make him feel better.

18. Because I can't fine someone to love me, I suspect there is something wrong with me.

19. Whenever I hear or read about husbands who cheat on their wives, I begin to fear that my boyfriend/husband is cheating on me.

20. I encourage my husband to function as head of the house, but he is irresponsible with money/parenting duties/drinking.

Make a note in your journal about the statements you marked very true or sometimes true. When you begin to use the SKILL Tools, you will be able to change this anxiety into constructive concern that leads to problem-solving action.

CHAPTER 5

◆ ◆ ◆

The Physiological Path to Worry

"Most people would say that I have nothing to worry about," Eve said in one of our focus groups. "I don't have a financial problem. I'm on good terms with my parents and friends. I've even made progress on my goal of growing spiritually. But I have no current love relationships and no clear focus about how I'm going to live the rest of my life. When something seems good to me, I can't seem to take action. Instead, I ask myself whether these are things I want to do, or whether they are ideas planted by my parents. I can't seem to make any decisions or come to a resolution about things. I feel like a leaf in a whirlpool being swirled around and around."

Approaching forty, Eve may be going through the anxiety that often hits both men and women as they examine where they've been and where they are going. She may be reacting with situational depression to the loss of past relationships and what she called "the first half of my life." Or, if a medical examination showed that she was low in estrogen, she could be walking along the Physiological Path to Worry. A lack of this important female hormone, which is often low during menopause and after a hysterectomy, can leave a woman feeling depressed, anxious, and worried for no reason that she can pinpoint. Furthermore, because of the actual anatomy of her brain, a woman may perceive more to worry about than a man might, given the same situation.

Are women really physiologically more susceptible to worry than men? The concept is controversial. No woman today wants to think that she could be victimized by "raging hormones." This idea is something that is all too easily used by others to trivialize women's feelings and justify holding them back from advancement. Yet, in his definitive book, *Beating Depression*, Dr. John Rush reports that two to three times as many women as men appear to be depressed at any given time. Studies show that this ratio holds across different cultures and is not affected by the degree to which women are "liberated."

Whether or not hormones really affect the behavior of women, our society says that they do. In 1986, the American Psychiatric Association proposed that a new category of mental illness—Pre-Menstrual Phase Dysphoric Disorder—be added to the *Diagnostic and Statistical Manual*, the mental health profession's "bible" for diagnosing and treating mental illnesses. Furthermore, during the eighties, juries judged that several women who killed their own infants were not guilty of murder; the legal defense was temporary insanity as a result of postpartum mental illness.

Few women react this severely to hormonal fluctuations, but many believe that hormones have an effect on them which is decidedly unpleasant. Some of our focus group members, for instance, reported feeling nervous and on edge or too tired to budge because of PMS (premenstrual stress syndrome).

"During the week before my period, I worry that I'm going to scream at my boss or break down and cry during a presentation," said one.

Elaine, a menopausal respondent, said that one night as she was frying chicken, she was feeling angry and weepy for no apparent reason. "When my husband asked how long it would be before supper was ready, it seemed to be the last straw. Something came over me and I just threw the skillet full of chicken out the back door into the yard. Then I went for a long walk to cool off, but all I could do was worry, 'What's wrong with me? Am I going crazy?' " she said.

Not all women react to the diminishing level of hormones during the change of life as Elaine did. A five-year study of more than 2,300 premenopausal women reported in the July 2, 1988, issue of *Science News* by Sonja M. McKinlay and John B. McKinlay of the New England Research Institute in Watertown, Massachusetts, showed that the depression sometimes associated with change of life is not due to physiological causes. Only 3 percent expressed any regret about their physical changes or loss of reproductive ability. Sonja McKinlay believed that this upbeat attitude was because the survey was based on healthy women. Those who were already depressed reported twice as many menopausal symptoms to their doctors as those who were not. The underlying causes of their depression stemmed largely from relationship issues.

Until scientists can agree on whether hormones can generate anxiety and depression, we believe that every woman should keep an open mind. Recognize that you could be one of those affected by your feminine anatomy but that you don't have to be a victim of monthly, change-of-life, or anatomical differences. Even if you worry because your body creates an anxious, worrisome mood, you can learn to cope with those changes—we'll explain how in chapter 14. Meanwhile, let's look in more detail at the following differences in a woman's body that can cause her to worry:

- *Hormonal differences.* As the levels of hormones fluctuate during the menstrual cycle, after childbirth, during menopause, and following a hysterectomy, women are subject to depression, anxiety, and other emotional reactions.
- *Differences in brain structure.* Some research concludes that female brain anatomy causes women to perceive the world with "wide-angle vision." Women simply perceive more to worry about.
- *Anatomical differences.* Women seem to have a greater physical predisposition to anxiety and panic attacks.

PMS-GENERATED WORRIES—
REAL OR IMAGINED?

Many medical professionals are convinced that hormonal fluctuations seven to ten days before a woman's menstrual period can cause transient blue moods. One popular theory, reported by Laura Claverie in the September 1987 issue of *Health* magazine, is that fluid retention brought on by increased estrogen levels just before menstruation causes not only breast tenderness and bloating but also somehow influences the brain and consequently women's moods. Larger premenstrual weight gains can increase the severity of PMS symptoms. Other researchers believe that women experience water retention, pain, and food cravings because they *expect* to do so before a period. The unconscious mind, they argue, creates the very symptoms women don't want!

We have a friend named Nita who is so affected by PMS that her husband writes "Nasty Nita" on his calendar on the week before her period. Then he tries to stay out of her way. Nita admits that she takes out her frustrations on her husband. When she is suffering from PMS, she says, she does all the hateful things she has stored up all month! We believe that Nita needs to ask her doctor for help in reducing the PMS symptoms. She should also consider the problems in her relationship with her husband and get help in solving them if that is necessary.

If PMS is a real problem for you, you can take action and overcome the anxiety that goes with it. Go to your doctor and ask for a complete evaluation. He or she may prescribe a combination of progesterone and vitamin B_6 to help you produce dopamine, a chemical that offsets anxiety. Watching what you eat the week before your period can help too. In the November 1988 issue of *Harper's Bazaar*, nutritionist Nan Kathryn Fuchs, Ph.D., of Santa Monica, advised PMS sufferers to follow a diet low in calcium, red meat, refined sugar, salt, caffeine, and alcohol. By eating more green, leafy vegetables and whole grains, you can avoid feeling run-down and tense.

TAKING THE HYSTERIA OUT OF HYSTERECTOMIES

One-third to one-half of American women will eventually have a total hysterectomy, surgical removal of the uterus alone, or a hysterectomy in conjunction with a bilateral oophorectomy, removal of both ovaries. The majority will be under the age of forty-four, according to Lynn Payer, author of *How to Avoid a Hysterectomy*. While the law requires that women be advised of the many possible side effects of having this major surgery, she found that few actually were. And one of the most common side effects of either type of hysterectomy may be depression. Her advice is to explore alternatives whenever possible.

As it is, however, millions of American women who have had hysterectomies are dependent on hormone replacement therapy to protect them from the same symptoms that women suffering from PMS or menopause report. As Jane well knows, the state of the medical art in prescribing such therapy often leaves a lot to be desired.

"I had a hysterectomy and bilateral oophorectomy in 1978," remembers Jane. "I started experiencing hot flashes and other menopausal symptoms, so in 1982 I was given estrogen replacement therapy. But the large doses of estrogen only made my mood swings worse. When I was blue, it seemed as if the world was coming to an end. I would become almost suicidal or so angry I was on the point of violence. I would ask myself why I was so distraught and attach the feeling to my marriage, my career, and just about anyone with whom I came in contact. When I was feeling good, I felt as high as a kite. I don't blame these mood swings entirely on the estrogen therapy, because I also was dealing with a failing marriage and an unwanted move to Texas. But I do believe that the estrogen accentuated my physiological condition."

In 1984, Jane found Dallas gynecologist Dr. John Woodward, who was participating in research that allowed him to use estrogen pellets. They were inserted under the skin to release a specific amount of estrogen over several months as the body requires.

"When I started telling Dr. Woodward about my worries, he said, 'I hear the same story all day every day from women who have had their ovaries removed and those who are menopausal or have PMS. I know exactly what happens to you.' Dr. Woodward was able to test me to see exactly how much estrogen I needed rather than just giving me a big dose and hoping that it met my needs. When he gave me the first pellet, I could tell the difference in the way I felt within twenty-four hours. I still have highs and lows because that's part of my personality, but they're now in a normal range," Jane says.

While estrogen pellets have not been approved for general use in the United States at the time of this writing, many other advancements in hormone replacement therapy are being made. If you have had a hysterectomy, you may want to explore whether your worries are heightened by improper hormonal levels.

MENOPAUSE AND WORRY

In our focus groups, women in their early thirties were already voicing fears of "growing old." Many in their forties said that aging was a big worry for them. And women of all ages were afraid of poor health or were beset by a vague feeling of "what's going to happen to me when I grow old?"

Aging is an issue that everyone must face, but women may worry about it more than men. At the very time when they must deal with the end of youth (which our culture holds sacred), they may be experiencing hot flashes, irritability, fatigue, insomnia, vaginal dryness that makes sex painful, and a decreased interest in sex.

For many, menopausal worries are a combination of physical discomforts and other issues. One forty-five-year-old single woman said, "I'm worried about my health. I have a new awareness of what it means to be middle-aged. I know people my age who have died or who have had cancer or heart disease. I worry about whether this could happen to me. If it does, how will I handle all this financially and who can I turn to for support? I would hope that I would make the best of whatever condition I may have, but at the same time I am aware that my resources at present are limited."

We believe that our SKILL Tools can help this woman overcome the helplessness and hopelessness that she is expressing. At the same time, many doctors are now recommending that every woman of menopausal age consider hormone replacement, whether she has any discomfort or not, according to a report by Kathleen McAuliffe in the May 23, 1988, issue of *U.S. News & World Report*. Such treatment may include estrogen, progesterone, and androgen in various combinations, depending on need. When correctly prescribed, hormone replacement therapy provides the physical benefit of staving off osteoporosis, a condition characterized by brittle bones and blamed for 2.5 million fractures in elderly women each year. It may help prevent cardiovascular disease by elevating the blood level of high-density lipoprotein (HDL), the "good" type of cholesterol, which helps keep arteries free of fatty deposits. Hormone replacement may also help women feel more vigorous and interested in sex, as well as relieve the vaginal dryness that causes painful intercourse.

Since hormone replacement has been shown to increase the risks of cancer for some women, Dr. Isaac Schiff, chief of gynecology at Massachusetts General Hospital in Boston, was quoted in *U.S. News & World Report* as saying that women contemplating taking hormones should have a medical evaluation. It should include a review of family history, a mammogram, a Pap smear, a blood-cholesterol test, and a bone-density evaluation. Women should be told about the risks so that they can make an educated decision about what is best for themselves.

The point is that women who are prone to worry because of menopausal changes may be able to alleviate some of the physical causes of their worry by taking action and looking into the possibility of medical intervention.

THE NEW BABY BLUES—PATH TO WORRY AND AGORAPHOBIA

When Angela Thompson of Sacramento started hearing the voice of God telling her her nine-month-old son was the devil, she drowned him in the bathtub, according to a report on postpartum depression in the June 20, 1988, issue of *Time* magazine. This tragedy occurred because she was one of the less than 1 percent of all new mothers who become psychotic after giving birth. Her legal defense was insanity as a result of postpartum mental illness, and a jury acquitted her.

How could the normal process of birth bring on insanity? During pregnancy, estrogen and progesterone increase a thousand-fold, then abruptly drop to normal or sometimes below normal after birth. Breast feeding is also accompanied by major hormonal changes. Between 50 percent and 80 percent of new mothers experience "new baby blues," becoming sensitive, moody, and tearful. While such feelings usually subside within a few weeks, about 8 percent to 12 percent suffer serious depressions, according to the *Time* article. These women undergo mercurial mood swings, lose their appetites, and go sleepless for nights on end. Thoughts of suicide or fantasies of killing their baby "are invasive, terrifying ideas that can drive them crazy," psychiatrist Ricardo Fernandez of Princeton, New Jersey, was quoted as saying in the article.

Adjusting to the demands of a new baby is difficult enough without the added trauma of hormonal fluctuations. If you are expecting a baby, recognize the possibility of experiencing postpartum depression. To protect yourself and your baby, you can ask for help from your doctor and from those around you. Our SKILL Tools are designed to help you be assertive so that you can meet your own needs when the baby comes. You will be able to take action to eliminate both the real danger and the worry that goes along with it.

While we know of no studies that associate childbirth with the development of agoraphobia, many women have told Bob that their first panic attack occurred when they were pregnant or shortly after giving birth to their first child, or after having major surgery. The stress of childbirth, surgery, or becoming a parent for the first time might be the factor that caused their anxiety level to overflow and precipitate the panic attack. We cannot help but wonder, however, whether the hormonal fluctuations after childbirth which are strong enough to cause postpartum depression might also be responsible for raising anxiety levels and precipitating panic attacks.

As we will show in chapter 15, some people have panic attacks because they are physically predisposed to panic and because they do not know how to manage their stress. In the presence of danger or high stress, their bodies more readily produce adrenaline which leads to anxiety, the fight or flight response, or panic. In women who do not know how to deal constructively with stress and whose adrenaline levels are already high, the physiological changes of childbirth could trigger the pituitary gland to produce even more adrenaline and thus a panic attack.

Women who are already agoraphobic may become even more anxious after childbirth, leaving us to wonder whether the change is caused by increased stress or a combination of stress and hormonal changes.

"Many agoraphobic women tell me they remember being afraid that they were going to harm their babies," Bob says. "They felt helpless and out of control. Being agoraphobic, they were overwhelmed with anxiety before giving birth. Afterward, they felt guilty that they couldn't take their babies outside in the sunshine or drive them to the doctor or even go to the store to buy diapers. This guilt and hidden anger increased their stress. At the same time, I wonder if the hormonal changes didn't also exacerbate their anxiety."

DO MEN AND WOMEN THINK DIFFERENTLY?

Only a century ago, scientists were trying to prove that women were born with intellectual and emotional weaknesses because their brains weighed less than those of men. Those myths were gradually debunked. Now researchers are looking at the different ways men and women use their right and left brains. In the aforementioned study by Christine de Lacoste-Utamsing and Ralph Holloway, a gender difference was found in the shape and surface area of the human corpus callosum—a large bundle of nerve fibers connecting the right and left hemispheres of the brain. As we noted, the researchers speculated that this difference could mean that women had more nerve fibers connecting the two hemispheres than men did, and hence women's brains were less lateralized or divided into separate right and left brain functions, than men's. In other words, the female brain hemispheres were less specialized, particularly for abstract spatial tasks such as mathematics, for which only one side of the brain is used. Specialization was not an overall advantage, however; these researchers also theorized that the reason why women register higher than men in verbal skills on performance tests is that women use *both* hemispheres while men use only *one*. Richard Restak, a neurologist at Georgetown University Medical School and author of *The Brain: The Last Frontier*, pointed out in the same *Science* article that this research could explain why more women than men who have had strokes recover their ability to speak. The unaffected side of a woman's brain takes over more readily.

"Anthropologists have speculated that brain lateralization also could mean that men and women have different perceptual systems," said Jim Wilson, the therapist who helped Bob recover from agoraphobia at the Phobia Center of the Southwest. "Men, who were the hunters in prehistoric times, developed 'tunnel vision' so that they could focus on the job of killing game. Women, who had to protect the children, developed 'wide-angle vision' in order to perceive dangers all around them. Today, this means that a husband and wife attending a cocktail party would remember different things about a conversation with another person. Using his 'tunnel vision,' the man would concentrate largely on what that person said. The woman, using her 'wide-angle vision,' would remember more details of the conversation as well as the clothes the other person wore and the room decor. At the same time, she might even pick up on other people's body language."

Anthropologist Mary Catherine Bateson, daughter of Margaret Mead, told Bill Moyers on the PBS program, "A World of Ideas," in 1988, "The traditional feminine roles as wife and mother of multiple children have involved caring for multiple issues, balancing them off, not neglecting that while you're caring about this, having one rhythm to respond to a husband and another one to an infant and another one to a growing child. This is what it is to be a woman . . . to keep a household going, to have multiple skills, to deal with transitions, to deal with the health of the whole. . . . You know what people say about women—that they're easily distracted, and that success has to do with focusing on specific goals. But what if the health of the world depends on the same kind of capacity that allows you, while you're feeding one child, to see that the other child is reaching up and about to pull a cooking pot of hot liquid on his head? This capacity to see out of the corner of your eye and care about the health, not just of one child but of three or four and a husband and other members of the family—that is the beginning of the capacity to care about the health of a multitude of nations, or an environment of many species."

With more input, women conceivably do have greater awareness of what is going on around them, but the disadvantage is that by having more data, they worry more. Furthermore, studies show that women are more inclined than men to link periods of self-analysis to periods of depression.

"When we feel down, we characteristically turn our mental energies inward through rumination, obsessive thought and worry," said Dr. Harriet Braiker in the March 1989 issue of *Lear's* magazine. "In contrast, men characteristically respond to feelings of sadness and depression by distracting themselves and shifting their attention onto work or other outside activities."

Meanwhile, the controversy over brain lateralization has not yet been settled. For every study that shows that women have lesser math and science capability than men, another "proves" that females have caught up with males. We believe that the brain is a very complicated organ whose operation is not yet clearly understood. If women have overcome their deficit in spatial skills and men have overcome their lag in verbal abilities, it doesn't necessarily mean that brain differences do not exist. Rather, it could mean that men and women have adapted to overcome these differences and have succeeded.

That is exactly what our SKILL Tools will help you do. You can learn to lessen your worries by mastering specific strategies that help you.

PRESCRIPTION DRUGS AND WORRY

While helping agoraphobics recover, Bob has seen that medications meant to ease anxiety sometimes actually increase it. And since more women than men seek professional help for panic attacks and depression, more women fall into the prescription drug trap. Here's how it works: A therapist prescribes a medication that blocks the body's response to fear, but does not require the patient to learn new ways of handling the stress that caused the panic reaction in the first place. The medication is often addictive if taken over a long period of time. Eventually the patient finds that not only is she dependent on the medication but the medication has side effects that are unpleasant. Now she has the worry of addiction in addition to the original worries that caused her panic attacks.

"While we believe that there is a physiological component to the onset of panic attacks," says Bob, "we do not believe that taking medication alone to block the feeling of fear is the best way to recover. It is important to understand that the discomfort of a panic attack comes from a normal condition—a fight or flight response. This response feels uncomfortable, but it is not going to hurt you. It's necessary to learn ways to desensitize yourself to your fears, and using diet and exercise can help your body feel normal. "It is my belief that if medication is used to alleviate fear symptoms, it should be used only as an adjunct to mastering the cognitive and behavioral techniques that will help you recover."

Women who seek medical treatment for depression may also be overmedicated, simply because they are female. In *The Good News About Depression*, Mark S. Gold, M.D., director of research at Fair Oaks Hospital, Summit, New Jersey, says that because many doctors believe hormones make females moody, they also feel that women have "weak constitutions." Seventy-five percent of all mood-altering drugs are prescribed to women, though they represent only 60 percent of the patients, according to Dr. Gold. Clearly some women, on the advice of their doctors, are taking pills to deal with their worries rather than learning the life skills that would help them more effectively. We think medication is part of a formula that guarantees continued anxiety.

PHYSIOLOGICAL CAUSES OF WORRY— DO YOU HAVE THEM?

To explore whether you are on the physiological path to worry, mark the following statements true or false:

                                                              True   False
_____

1. More stressful things seem to happen during the week before my period than at other times during the month.

True   False

2. Discomfort from water retention before my period makes it difficult for me to sleep.

3. People tell me that I'm hard to get along with before my period even though I don't think that I am.

4. I get embarrassed when I have a hot flash in public.

5. I have a lot of minor physical problems in connection with my period that make it impossible for me not to be irritable.

6. Sometimes I just feel blue for no reason at all.

7. I used to feel cheerful most of the time, but now there are times when I have so many worries that I can't help but feel down.

8. Since my hysterectomy I often lose my temper and snap at others.

9. Since my hysterectomy I sleep too much or not enough.

10. Since my hysterectomy I have violent mood swings.

11. I worry about getting old more than my friends of the same age do.

12. After my baby was born, I was so tired and impatient all the time that I was afraid I was going to hurt her.

13. After my baby was born, I started feeling jittery about going places without my husband, so now I just stay at home.

14. My boyfriend/husband says that I'm making up things to worry about, but he doesn't see all the things that I see.

15. I want to keep up with my old interests, but I feel too nervous and distracted at certain times to pursue them.

16. I worry because sex isn't nearly as much fun as it used to be—sometimes it's actually painful.

There are no right or wrong answers in this quiz. It is an opportunity to consider whether you are worrying without being fully aware that your body exacerbates your anxiety or may even be the cause of it. Consider your answers and then think about your worries during the past three months. Did any of the physical conditions you marked true affect your mood? Did any of them actually begin the worry process? Or keep it going once it started? If so, make a note for future reference. Write out your experiences in your journal.

When Bob had agoraphobia, he helped himself get off the worry-go-round by setting a goal to improve his nutrition and fitness levels. Since caffeine stimulates the adrenal glands to produce anxiety-causing hormones, for instance, he found he could remain calmer by eliminating coffee from his diet. Running caused his body to produce endorphins, the body's natural painkillers, which in turn elevated his mood. Getting off the Physiological Path to Worry helped him recover from the fears that kept him housebound. We believe that you can do the same. The chapters that follow provide the SKILL Tools for getting off the worry-go-round once and for all.

PART II

◆ ◆ ◆

Mastering the SKILL Tools

CHAPTER 6

◆ ◆ ◆

The First SKILL Tool:
Seek the Real Reason for
Your Worry

We have described the four paths that cause women to get caught in the worry trap, because we want you to understand how emotions, instincts, societal pressures, and physical problems lead you to climb aboard the worry-go-round. In this part of the book, you will learn five SKILL Tools for getting off the worry-go-round and then finding the pearl in your worries. These tools have already helped thousands of women do just that. We urge you to study them carefully and then apply them to yourself.

The first SKILL Tool is designed to help you discover the same reality noted by scientists who studied the atom. In about 400 B.C., the Greek philosopher Democritus theorized that if matter were divided into finer and finer pieces, it would eventually reach a point where it could no longer be divided. He called this smallest bit of matter an atom, and for more than two-thousand years no one believed that anything could be smaller. After all, an atom is so tiny if couldn't be seen—not even after the electron microscope was invented. With the new tool of mass spectrometry, however, scientists discovered that each atom was large enough to contain a nucleus made up of several kinds of particles. In fact, atoms were like miniature solar systems, with galaxies of information still unknown.

In the same way that scientists are making new discoveries about something they thought they understood, you, by using our first SKILL Tool, may discover that your worries are far different from what you think they are:

◆ *The First SKILL Tool: Seek the Real Reason for Your Worry.*

Using this tool, you can function like a physician who considers every clue in order to make a definitive diagnosis. Once you know what the real problem is, the other four tools will teach you to formulate the right "prescription" for healing your worry.

Before Bob developed agoraphobia, he worried about his business, his family, and the impression he made on others. Everyone called him a successful entrepreneur, but he worried that he wasn't making as much money as some other people he knew. When his mother was grieving over the death of his father, he worried that he wasn't a good son because he couldn't make her stop being sad. In front of his friends, he put on the mask of being "good old Bob, a fun-loving guy," but inside he worried that others would find out that he was nothing but an insecure failure. All of these worries added to the stress that was filling up his rain barrel. When it spilled over, he started having panic attacks.

While Bob was recovering from agoraphobia, he gave himself permission to become introspective. How did he become such a negative thinker? Why did he feel that he had to control the behavior of other people in order to be a "good" person? Why couldn't he accept the fact that he was a successful businessman without putting himself down and looking for disaster just around the corner? Why did he fear both failure and success? After much study, he discovered the hidden agenda of his worry: He had a poor self-image that grew out of the trauma caused by having a withered leg as a child.

At this point Bob had both the diagnosis and the prescription for getting off the worry-go-round and seeking the pearl in his worry. The diagnosis was poor self-esteem. The prescription was to improve his self-esteem by nurturing that little child within him and changing the negative way he talked about himself to himself. Bob took this "medicine" by concentrating his thoughts on his self-worth and positive qualities. He found it went down easily. It helped block his panic attacks and opened the way for a new career. It also brought him a revelation about the way he felt about others: When he had been on the worry-go-round, he was too engrossed in his own problems to be able to love others uncondi- tionally. Now he felt competent and empowered to reach out to others in a wonderful way he had never known before. This entirely new outlook on life he called Life Plus.

Look deep within yourself and you may find that the real reason you worry is that you have a hidden or unconscious agenda that causes you to manufacture worrying behavior.

THE "THREE LACKS" IN A WOMAN'S HIDDEN AGENDA

Like Bob, the women in our focus groups who considered them- selves chronic worriers discovered hidden agendas that generated worrying behavior. The items on these hidden agendas were so similar among so many women that we started calling them the "Three Lacks." We've since become convinced that most women who worry suffer from a:

- *Lack of self-esteem.* Feeling that the face you present others is not your true self, and that if anyone discovered the real you, they would reject you.
- *Lack of confidence.* Feeling unable to cope because you have had no encouragement in risking or doing unfamiliar things.
- *Lack of ability to make decisions and solve problems.* Feeling help- less, passive and resentful.

You may have these Three Lacks without recognizing them. You may simply tell yourself that you worry because you have no control over what is happening to you. For instance, if your father falls ill, you may tell yourself that it is natural to be concerned about his health. If you lose your job, you may tell yourself there is little else you can do except lie awake at night and wonder how you are going to make the next car payment. If your son is failing at school, you may give in to fantasizing about his future in a shelter for the homeless. Worry in this way can only harm you. Recognize that if the situation is truly beyond your control, you can use the Fifth SKILL Tool to learn to let go of these worries. Don't be too quick to use it, however, because you can do more than let go. If your father is sick, you can first take constructive action by exploring alternatives for his medical care. If you lose your job, you can borrow money, look for another job, or decide to sell your car and use public transportation. If your son makes bad grades, you can find a tutor.

WHAT'S YOUR WORRY THEME?

When you *fail to take action* in situations like these you may suspect that one of the Three Lacks has taken over and is creating what we call a *worry theme*. These phrases often characterize worry themes:

"What if . . . ?"
"How will . . . ?"
"I can't . . ."
"I don't know how I . . ."
"It's all my fault . . ."
"Why can't I . . . ?"
"Why won't he/she . . . ?"
"I'm such a bad . . ."
"How did I get to be . . . ?"
"What will others think if . . . ?"
"Why didn't I . . . ?"
"I should/ought to . . ."

Lack of self-esteem might cause you to build a worry theme around your child's school failure that includes statements to yourself such as, "*It's my fault* he's going to drop out of school." "*Why can't I* make him study?" "*Why won't he* listen to me?" "*I'm such a bad* mother."

If your father is sick, for example, you may agonize, *"What if* I can't take care of him? *What if* he has to go to a nursing home and *what if* I can't pay for it? *What if* no one else will help me?" This worry theme is one that starts with your father's illness but spirals into your own lack of confidence. Before you know it you are on the worry-go-round.

Lack of decision-making and problem-solving skills might cause you to build a worry theme around losing your job that includes *"How will I* get to work if I don't have a car?" *"I can't* live on less money," and *"I don't know how* I will get another job." If you weren't trained as a child to be assertive, you may be afraid to compete for a new or better job. The phrases "How will I?," "I can't," and "I don't know how" betray this lack of confidence that makes it hard for you to take action.

By exploring your worry themes and identifying when and where the Three Lacks appear, you can diagnose the true nature of your worry. Then you can take action, not only to solve the immediate problem and rid yourself of the worry but also to increase your self-esteem, self-confidence, and problem-solving and decision-making skills. This is the path to pearl worry, and the First SKILL Tool is the way to begin the process.

When Jane was writing her thesis for her master's degree, she couldn't get started. Every time she sat in front of the typewriter, she panicked. *"I should be able* to write it but I can't." *"Why am I such a bad* writer?" *"What if I never* get started?" *"What if I fail* to get my master's degree?" She felt that the thesis was completely out of her control. She was so lacking in self-confidence that she couldn't write a word. Then she asked a professor for help. "Sit down and write, 'I can't write this, I'm not getting my mind together,' " he advised. "Keep on writing until you finally get out all your fear and anxiety. Then you will be able to start. Write at least one page every day." Jane took his advice and eventually wrote her thesis, one page at a time.

To identify which one of the Three Lacks is causing you to worry rather than take action, write down the "mental chatter" you have about the worrisome situation. What are the questions that you are asking yourself? What judgments or assumptions are you making? Are any of them on the worry list above? Do they indicate a lack of self-esteem, self-confidence, or not knowing how to make decisions and solve problems? If so, set your goal to overcome these lacks. Find small ways to take action so that you will have some control over the situation.

For instance, you can make a list of your good qualities and read them over every morning to increase your self-esteem. You can take courses or get counseling or talk over a problem with a friend to increase your confidence about risking new behavior. You can check yourself to see whether you are taking some small action every day that will lead toward reaching a long-range goal.

Now let's look once again at the four pathways to worry. This time, ask yourself if any of the hidden agendas described are causing you to build a worry theme. Write your worry theme down in your journal. Then study the other four SKILL Tools to learn what you can do to overcome it.

PSYCHOSOCIAL HIDDEN AGENDAS

"During my first marriage," remembers Jane, "I never asked for what I really wanted. I was only nineteen years old when I got married. I also had low self-esteem because of my scars. Furthermore, as a southerner, I was brought up to believe that it wasn't right for a woman to ask for what she wanted. The model for me in *Gone with the Wind* was sweet Melanie, not fiery Scarlett O'Hara! Melanie suffered a lot but she was always sweet and brave, she never asked anything of anybody. Everybody loved Melanie; she was so kind and good. The only problem was that when I tried to live like Melanie, I felt resentment twenty-four hours a day. I developed a worry theme about my husband, my son, and myself that just never went away. It was as if a voice inside of me said, 'If I don't get their approval and love, they might abandon me, and then I'll die.' "

After her divorce, Jane didn't know about the First SKILL Tool, but she did go through a lot of therapy. She learned that she was a worthy person who deserved to tell others how she really felt. "When I began dating Bob, I deliberately put my *worst* foot forward. If I didn't like something, I said so. Then I would wait for an explosion that never happened. Gradually I learned to trust my own responses. I learned that I could disagree with someone and survive. Even when I felt afraid that others wouldn't agree with my opinion or my request, it was still all right for me to express it." Jane doesn't have the worries and resentments she used to have.

If you have been recording information about yourself in your journal as we advised, you may already have some insight into why and how you worry. Take a moment now to review any life experiences you recorded which you believe may have caused you to follow the Psychosocial Path to Worry.

Now consider whether any of these experiences might cause you to answer yes to the following questions:

- Do you worry about how you look or how others see you?
- Do you worry that others might discover who the real you is?
- Does a critic in your head tell you you're not doing a good enough job at anything you do?
- Do you let high-pressure salespeople sell you an outfit that you know does nothing for you and then feel resentful?
- Are you afraid to tell others what you really think because you might lose their friendship or love?
- Do you refrain from asking for what you want, then feel angry when you don't get it?

Do your answers reflect a perception of yourself as unworthy, a fraud, or somehow not as good as others? If so, you yourself may be the one who stands in the way of freedom from worry. Write a promise to yourself in your journal that you will work to increase your self-esteem. Write several affirmations about yourself. For instance, you might write the following:

- It's okay for me to work on increasing my self-esteem.
- Liking myself will make me less demanding of myself and others.
- When I can reveal what I want, I open the way for true closeness with those I love.

If you answered no to the questions above, the childhood experiences you have written about may not be the reason for your worry; your perception of them has not caused you to lack confidence or self-esteem. You may simply need to learn problem-solving and decision-making skills.

INSTINCTIVE HIDDEN AGENDAS

Felicia, a divorced teacher, told her focus group that she worries a lot about her three grown children. "If one of them telephones me at night, my first thought is that they've had an accident, they're hurt, they don't have any insurance, and it's going to cost me a fortune. It's as if it is up to me to solve and pay for all their problems. I can see this worry going on forever. If one of them should get married and have a child, I'll probably have to worry about it, too! I know it sounds as if I'm overprotective, because after all, my children are in their twenties. But when they get into trouble, I can't just say, 'I don't care,' as my parents did about me. I was dumped by my folks. So, I'll spend all my money on my kids. I'll keep on doing it forever."

Felicia's maternal instincts are out of control. Even though she knows she is crippling her children by rescuing them from the consequences of their actions, she can't stop. The key to why she can't is her statement, "I was dumped as a child." She still thinks of herself as a rejected, needy little child who was somehow so unlovable that no one took care of her. Since she was such a "bad little girl," she can't nurture herself, only her children. All the caring she wishes that she had received she gives to her kids because she is not worthy to have it herself. She is also overcompensating to make sure that she never does to her own children what her parents did to her.

If Felicia's children do get into trouble, Felicia could easily be tagged as the codependent who helped make it all happen. And, Felicia is causing herself a lot of worries she doesn't have to take on.

Look at the notes you wrote in your journal after taking the quiz in chapter 3 on the Instinctive Path to Worry. We asked you to record incidents in your childhood that might have converted your nurturing instincts into the urge to climb aboard the worry-go-round. Ask yourself these questions:

- Have these incidents caused me to feel that it is my responsibility to solve other people's problems?
- Do I feel guilty if I spend time, energy, or money on myself instead of on work or on others?
- Is it hard for me to say no?

If you have determined that your nurturing instincts have led you into the worry trap, you almost certainly lack self-esteem. You may also need to learn problem-solving and decision-making skills in order to become more assertive. As you master the SKILL Tools, you will fulfill these needs.

SOCIETAL HIDDEN AGENDAS

Fran, the manager of a small store, indignantly told Jane how badly she had been treated by a serviceman at an automotive repair shop, not realizing that she was describing her own lacks that caused her to walk down the Societal Path to Worry.

"One morning I discovered that my car had two flat tires, so I asked my husband to put air in the tires. Then I drove to the automotive shop. I told the serviceman, 'My hub caps have locks on them, so you must use the lock tool which is in the trunk of my car to take them off. Here are my keys. Be sure to use the special tool.' He promised he would do that and have the car ready in two hours. When I returned, he hadn't even started, but he said he would finish the job in another hour. The next time I returned, the hubcaps were lying on the floor bent out of shape. I was angry, but all I said was, 'Didn't you use the lock tool?' He replied, 'I didn't need to. They were wobbly and came off easily.' How could they have, as bent as they were? I was so furious, I just walked out. When I returned, I paid for the service and drove home with my misshapen hubcaps.

"When my husband saw the hubcaps he insisted that we drive back to the service station immediately. He demanded that the manager replace my hubcaps, and the manager agreed to do so. Once again I left my car there. When I returned, the seviceman told me he hadn't been able to get the same kind of hubcaps, so he had hammered out the dents. My hubcaps still looked terrible, but

I was so frustrated I simply drove home. Now I'm worried that my husband will be angry at me for not sticking up for myself. What's wrong with me? Why couldn't I stand up to that seviceman? I just let people walk all over me."

Jane pointed out that Fran would have been the first to try to satisfy an unhappy customer in her own shop, yet she had not asserted herself with the seviceman who had ruined her hubcaps. Moreover, Fran was afraid to tell her husband what she had done. With some introspection, Fran saw that the reason for her lack of assertiveness with men stemmed from having been an abused child. She had so desperately needed her father's love while she was growing up that she turned her anger on herself rather than on her abusive father. She told herself that she must have been bad or he wouldn't hurt her. Fran grew up thinking that her role as a woman was to be "nice," i.e., subservient to men. In fact, given her abuse, being nice was—to the little child within—the only way to survive. Thus she passively allowed men to take advantage of her. In addition, since society had molded her, as a female, *not* to solve problems and make decisions, she depended on her husband to do that for her.

Now review your answers to the quiz in chapter 4 on the Societal Path to Worry. Do the statements that you marked "very true" or "sometimes true" reflect a lack of self-esteem, confidence, or problem-solving and decision-making abilities? If so, write a paragraph in your journal stating any insights you may have received and how you can change.

Here is what Fran might write: "Because of having been abused as a child, I often let men take advantage of me. I will work to improve my self-esteem by writing down the many good things that are true about me and making a list of affirmations. Whenever I feel angry that a man is mistreating me, I will remind myself that I am a worthy person who deserves to be treated well. It is perfectly all right for me to speak up to any man. I will practice an assertive reply and then say it to him. I will ask my husband to remind me to do this whenever I complain about being put down by a man."

THE PHYSIOLOGICAL HIDDEN AGENDAS

Dawn told her focus group that her hysterectomy marked the start of trouble with worry. "Ever since that operation, I frequently get headaches. One morning, I woke up with a headache because the people in the apartment above me had partied noisily all night. I stayed home from work worrying about what I was going to do. I needed to get out of that noisy apartment, but I wondered about buying that house I had been looking at. All my friends told me not to buy it, that it wasn't a good deal, but somehow, as I lay there, I kept thinking, 'All your life you've let other people make your decisions for you. Are you just going to give in again?' Headache and all, I got out of bed, called the realtor and finalized the deal. Later, I discovered my friends were right. The neighborhood was terrible. Furthermore, the house was just as noisy as the apartment, because it was located on the approach to an airport several miles away. Jets were always roaring overhead. I realized I had made a terrible mistake. How could I have screwed up so badly? Now I worry a lot about *that*, but I blame it on the headaches. If I could just think clearly, maybe I wouldn't make mistakes," she said.

Dawn's hysterectomy may have been responsible for the mood swings, irritability, headaches, and other physical problems that started her down the Physiological Path to Worry. Dawn would do well to ask her doctor to test her for hormonal replacement therapy. If she felt better, would she be able to make better decisions for herself? Perhaps. She might make even better ones if she increased her self-esteem. Dawn needs to realize that while buying that particular house was a mistake, her decision to take action was not. She was simply doing what anyone who solves problems must do—taking a risk, which in itself is commendable. If one takes a risk under physical duress like a headache or out of a sense of low self-esteem (such as when Dawn asked herself, "*Why can't I* decide this for myself?"), failure is more likely. This is why learning to take care of the self—both body and psyche—is part of the SKILL Tool program. If Dawn made a mistake, the next rational step was not to scold herself but to look at the alternatives for improving her health and self-esteem—and risk again.

Now look at what you wrote in your journal after taking the quiz in chapter 5 on the Physiological Path to Worry. Did your worry themes really begin with hormonal fluctuations? If so, did any of the Three Lacks play a part? Try writing about these worries again and see if any of the Lacks "fit." If so, make a note for future reference.

Dawn's observations might look like this: "I made a mistake because I rebelled against the advice of friends who wanted to help me and because I made a decision when I had a headache. I know that I tend to rebel against authority because my mother always insisted that I do things her way and she made decisions for me. In the future, whenever I feel myself being impulsive, I will tell myself that I deserve to benefit from good advice. I will affirm that I am a worthy person. I will also go to the doctor and ask for help with my headaches. I will try not to make important decisions when I have a headache."

THE "SO WHAT?" TECHNIQUE

When the OPEC nations limited the supply of oil to the United States in the midseventies, the millions of auto owners who had to wait in line for gasoline were especially sensitive to rumors about shortages. Just how sensitive they were, Johnny Carson discovered. One night in his monologue, he joked, "The next thing they'll say is that there's a shortage of toilet paper in Los Angeles." Everyone laughed, but by the next day Los Angeles newspapers reported that not a roll of toilet paper could be found on supermarket shelves. Apparently the word "shortage" pressed worry buttons for a lot of people who reacted, joke or not.

Even though we hope that doing the exercises in this chapter has helped you become more introspective, you may still not feel that you have discovered your hidden agendas for worry. You may tell yourself that you are simply worried about such things as being fifteen pounds overweight, or being afraid that your husband is having an affair, or that someone might break into your house, or that you are angry that you haven't had a raise in three years. "These are just the facts," you might say. "There is no hidden agenda."

Sometimes, however, the truth is so painful that your unconscious protects you from it. All it has to do is hear you ask yourself, "But what is *really* true?" and it reacts with the speed of the toilet-paper shoppers of Los Angeles with self-protective actions. It tells you being overweight or afraid that your husband is having an affair has nothing to do with the fact that you had a miserable childhood which led to a lack of self-esteem. Being angry over not getting a raise does not relate to the fact that you were never encouraged to solve your own problems when you were a little girl, and that you lack confidence to solve them now.

Psychologists call this phenomenon "denial," and we have a way to deal with it: the "So What?" Technique. Bob got this idea from participating in a sales seminar. The salespersons sat in a circle. When the instructor threw the ball to one of them, he or she caught it, threw it back, and gave the sales spiel about the product. Then the instructor would throw the ball back while everyone yelled, "So what?" The salesperson would have to think of something even better to say about the product. This "So What?" process was repeated over and over. The salespersons in the circle thought of more reasons why customers should buy their product than they ever believed possible.

You can do the same thing when you are trying to figure out a hidden agenda for your worry. Here is the process:

1. Write down what you think is the real reason for your worry. Then ask yourself, "So what?" Write down any thoughts that come to you.
2. Go deeper. Ask yourself if you might have a different reason, one that stems from your feelings. Write it down. Then ask yourself, "So what?"
3. Go even deeper. Check out the Three Lacks, even though you may not think they apply to you. If they apply, write down how they apply. Continue repeating the process until you simply cannot think of any other reason.
4. Now look at what you wrote. Congratulate yourself that you are using the First SKILL Tool.
5. Write down a goal to overcome any lacks in yourself that are causing you to worry.

Teri was often angry about the put-downs from her teenage stepdaughter, Vicki. As a child, Teri had parents who doted on her older sister. Every time that her husband sided with his hostile daughter against her, she felt the same anger and sense of rejection that she had experienced as a little girl when her father ignored her accomplishments. In an attempt to win Vicki over, Teri cooked Vicki's favorite foods and even allowed the girl to leave her room in a mess rather than keep it neat, but nothing seemed to work. Teri kept asking herself, "Why can't that girl change?" and "What if she destroys my relationship with my husband?" She was positive that the source of her worry was in Vicki. Then Teri used the "So What?" Technique. Here is her dialogue:

"The real reason for my worry is that Vicki doesn't like me."
"So what?"
"So I don't like it when Vicki puts me down."
"So what?"
"So I feel hurt."
"So what?"
"So whenever I feel hurt, I get angry. Because I don't have very good self-esteem, I tend to lash out at others instead of discussing my feelings."
"So what!"
"So it's good that I now recognize the problem. I will set a goal of getting some professional help to deal with it."

Then Teri remembered that whenever her sister won another award, Teri felt hurt and lashed out at everyone. This kind of behavior didn't win *her* any awards! She often felt unloved and a failure. Teri realized that she had cast Vicki as her rival sibling. When Vicki hurt her, she replayed her childhood memories and lashed out at her husband in return. Teri sought family counseling to deal with her own lack of self-esteem and to help Vicki relate to her as a mother. She set goals to build her self-esteem that included affirmations such as, "Even if Vicki doesn't like me, I am still a person of worth." By taking action, she solved her worries.

After applying the "So What?" technique, it may be that you have not found any hidden motives. There are times when people worry simply because life is hard. One woman in our focus groups worried because she had lost her business and gone bankrupt. Another mourned because her child had died. By using the "So What?" Technique in these situations, you will see that you have no hidden agenda. These are severe losses over which grieving is appropriate.

THE TRUTH ABOUT YOUR WORRIES

Bob's first wife, Cindy, told us that she was depressed for three years before their divorce. "What's wrong with me? Why do I feel so miserable?" she kept asking herself. The truth of the matter was that Cindy denied to herself a very painful truth: She was afraid to acknowledge feelings which were somehow unacceptable. One of those was that she no longer loved her husband. When she finally admitted that and got her divorce, she began learning to recognize how she really felt. Her depression and the accompanying worries lifted.

We hope that you can see the importance of seeking the real reasons for your worry. When you use the wrong prescription, you cannot heal an illness; you must first have the proper diagnosis.

We've told this story before, but we think it is the perfect example of what happens when you perceive the wrong information about a situation. It is about the man who walked into a small-town cafe and noted the headline on a newspaper that was lying on a chair. "Hard times are coming," it said. This customer didn't know that the newspaper was an old one that the owner of the cafe had found tucked away on a dusty shelf and was going to throw away. He panicked. "If hard times are coming, I'd better not build that house I wanted," he told himself. He called the construction company and said, "Hard times are coming. I'm going to cancel my order." The construction company owner thought, "Hard times? I'd better cancel my order for lumber." When he did, the lumber company laid off workers. Soon the whole town was paralyzed with genuine hard times, all because one man had perceived the truth differently from what it was.

Don't become convinced that your worries are insurmountable and that there is nothing you can do about them. Talk about how awful they are. Use the First SKILL Tool to get at their cause. When you are finished writing in your journal, proceed to the Second SKILL Tool in chapter 7. It will help you get off the worry-go-round and on the way to finding the pearl in your worry.

CHAPTER 7

◆ ◆ ◆

The Second SKILL Tool:
Know Your Alternatives

"I got ten solid offers after receiving my MBA," Gail told her focus group, "but the one I accepted turned out to be nothing but a shark's nest. Right away I could tell that something was terribly wrong in that company, but what was it? Was *I* the problem? Every single day I got nothing but rejection and negative feedback. I was too inexperienced to have any coping skills, and I had moved to a strange city where I had no friends whom I could ask for advice. I was frozen with worry, but I was determined to succeed, so I started working ninety hours a week. Then I got fired! It was like having a midlife crisis at twenty-three. I was so depressed that I didn't get another job for almost a year."

Nine years later, Gail could see that the situation at the company where she first worked was abnormal. Getting fired had little to do with her competency, but she hadn't been able to shake off the effect. "I had always been something of a perfectionist. I was considered a 'whiz kid' at college. Being fired from that first job really took something out of me. I've done nothing but worry on the job ever since. I keep telling myself, 'Watch out! Don't mess up!' As a result, I haven't progressed as far as I could."

Gail has already used the First SKILL Tool: She knows that the reason for her worry is not only the trauma of being fired, but also her perfectionistic nature and a lack of self-esteem and confidence. Yet she is still on the worry-go-round as far as her work is concerned. Why? Like many women who worry compulsively, Gail is problem-oriented rather than solution-oriented. When she is with other women, she keeps ruminating on the past and painting fearsome scenarios for the future. Her friends try to console her by telling war stories of their own, but no one suggests alternative actions that could produce solutions. Telling war stories only reinforces worry and low self-esteem.

Our Second SKILL Tool breaks problem-oriented thinking by showing you ways that you can move towards solution. It is simply this:

◆ *The Second SKILL Tool: Know Your Alternatives.*

When you become aware that you have alternatives, you can choose the best one and start taking action to eliminate the lacks you discovered by working with the First SKILL Tool. Worriers often don't even see alternatives, however, because alternatives mean a change in behavior and hardly anyone welcomes that. Yet, if you look back on your life, you will find that your periods of most significant growth probably came about because you were forced to change.

When Bob had agoraphobia, he brainstormed with solution-oriented phobics about alternative ways of living that would help him recover. To overcome his lack of self-esteem, he visualized himself as he wanted to be and affirmed that he was already that way. To feel better physically, he had to stop drinking alcohol and coffee and start eating healthfully. "I had known that I needed to make those changes, but I resisted until I had to choose between making them or having panic attacks," Bob remembers. By mastering the Second SKILL Tool, you can discover opportunities to find the pearl of new choices and options that can arise from your worry.

THE "TRIPLE A" FORMULA FOR BECOMING SOLUTION-ORIENTED

Maybe you believe that you've already sought out alternatives and that none of them has made you worry any less. If so, then you need to dig for more alternatives! Our "Triple A" Formula will help do just that. Like that other famous Triple A, the American Automobile Association, this formula provides peace of mind and freedom from anxiety. When a breakdown occurs, it offers emergency care.

The A's in our formula stand for Alter, Avoid, and Accept. To use the formula, think about your worry scenario and then ask yourself which of the three A's you can use to find solution-oriented alternatives:

- Can you *alter* your scenario so that it will be less worrisome? Our techniques for altering worries are to brainstorm, use time management, learn to say "I'm not willing," and to challenge "what if" thinking—all to be explained shortly.
- Can you *avoid* the forces that cause you to worry in the first place? Our techniques for preventing worry include avoiding "worry partners," distracting yourself and saying no to Mr. Negative.
- Can you *accept* the worry scenario and learn to live with it? Some worries are facts of life that you cannot change. We will teach you how to change your attitude so that you can let go of worries over which you have no control.

BRAINSTORMING ALTERNATIVES

To use the altering approach to worry, sit down with a blank piece of paper divided into two columns, one labeled "Worry" and the other "Alternatives." Write down your worry scenario in the first column and ideas about how you can act differently in the second. For instance, you may write down, "I am worrying about how I am going to get a leaky faucet repaired." In the second column, you can write, "I will call a plumber" as the first solution and "I will do it myself" as the second. If you feel you can't do it yourself but don't have money to pay the plumber, write, "I am worrying about how to pay the plumber," in the first column. In the second, you might then write, "I'll put off buying something else," or "I'll budget more carefully this month." By the time you have put all this on paper, you will have several alternatives from which you can choose the best and get on with the action. By moving to solution, you will worry less.

If you have exhausted all your ideas and still haven't found a workable alternative, or if you have a chronic worry or one that has kept you in knots for as long as two days, you may need the help of others. If so, call or gather together an objective group of action-oriented friends, present your worry situation, and ask them to brainstorm solutions. "Storming the brains" of several people creates synergy—a "super mind," which is capable of producing a better solution than any individual could. Like a thunderstorm that crackles with electricity and power, a good brainstorm bounces ideas back and forth like bolts of lightning. It produces a lot of rain that generates growth.

We must warn you, however, that it is important to select the right kind of people with whom to brainstorm. Jane says, "I've been in groups where the only response to my concern was, 'Oh, that happened to you? Well let me tell you what happened to *me*!' Three hours later we were still telling 'poor me' stories. We were still thinking about problems rather than solutions." Don't choose friends who will listen to your worries, and then play the "ain't it awful" game by telling war stories of their own.

Here are seven steps for successful brainstorming;

1. *Select objective brainstormers.* Unfortunately, family members may be too emotionally involved with you to generate the best alternatives. Instead, find people who will, like a good therapist, listen to your concerns but not allow you to wallow in them. You can ask friends you trust, members of a support group, or professionals.

2. *If your problems require expertise, choose knowledgeable brainstormers.* To find alternatives to career worries, consider objective coworkers, individuals whose achievements you admire, or more experienced people in your field who might be willing to serve as mentors. If you are worried about your children, seek out the counsel of other parents, teachers, or pediatricians.

3. *Set out the ground rules*. Explain that you don't want pity but rather good, objective solutions.

4. *Encourage people to say anything that pops into their mind*. Sometimes the most farfetched suggestions are just what you need to get unstuck from a cycle of negative thinking. They may also generate an idea in your mind that isn't so ridiculous.

5. *Have someone write down or tape the ideas.*

6. *Avoid comments like "yes, but . . ."* When someone gives you a suggestion, just thank them and write it down.

7. *Review the entire brainstorming session in private*. Choose what you consider are the three best alternatives.

Remember that you can also brainstorm with good self-help books and tapes. And you can get ideas from workshops and seminars. Bob found many alternatives from such sources that helped him recover from agoraphobia. Look to any source of information, living or inanimate, that will help generate ideas.

THE THREE-D TIME-MANAGEMENT TECHNIQUE

Women in our focus groups said they worried because they didn't have enough time to accomplish everything they felt they had to do. While at the office they couldn't get their work done because they were worrying about who was picking up the kids or how they would find time to buy groceries or how they could get the sofa reupholstered when no one was at home to wait for the serviceperson. At home they accomplished less than they wanted to because they worried about that report they just couldn't get started writing at the office.

In chapter 3, we showed how the society we live in really does demand superhuman achievements from women. Harried lifestyles generate a lot of anxiety. Our Three-D Time-Management Technique is a strategy for altering the way you race the clock so you don't have to worry about accomplishing less than you would like. All you have to do is to look at your list of tasks and categorize them as "do its", "drop its", or "delegate its." Here's how it works:

1. As early as possible every morning, sit down with a pencil and piece of paper and write a list of everything you want to accomplish that day.

2. Decide those tasks that you can *realistically* do in the next twenty-four hours. Write "do it" beside these entries.

3. Decide which entries are unfeasible and write "drop it" beside them. Perhaps you haven't the money to reupholster the sofa now. Your worry about what others will think about your house is only harming you. Give yourself permission to drop that worry for today and put your energy into accomplishing the "do it" tasks.

4. Decide which entries others can do, and write "delegate it." Be creative and assertive. You might develop a car pool to pick up the children or pay a neighbor to perform this chore for you, for instance. You might negotiate with your husband a method of sharing the chore of buying groceries. If a voice in your head tells you that by delegating you are shirking your "duties," remind yourself that you are a worthy person who deserves all the help she can get.

5. Now go back to the "do its" and number them, according to priority. If a task seems overwhelming to you, break it down into small steps and complete it in steps. For instance, if you have a report that you just can't seem to start writing, set a goal of writing only two pages of it today. Give yourself permission to turn out less than Nobel Prize quality.

6. Work to accomplish all of the "do its' in twenty-four hours. When Jane was a teacher, she discovered that whether she told the children they had ten minutes or two hours to do an assigned task in the classroom, they always finished it. If you know that you have a time limit, you will likely achieve your do its.

Geri, a business consultant, told us that the Three-D Time-Management Technique helped her see that she had been sabotaging herself whenever she called prospects. "I was spending a lot of time calling people I knew weren't going to use my services, simply because I knew they were easy to talk to. When I used the Three-D Time-Management Technique, I decided to write "drop it" beside all those calls that would be unproductive. When I started writing 'do it' beside prospects I had been avoiding, I started making more money and worrying less," she said.

THE "I'M NOT WILLING" TECHNIQUE

Greta told her focus group that when her five brothers and sisters started having children, her grandmother just couldn't afford to buy Christmas presents for everyone. The older woman suggested that members of the family draw names and buy one nice present for the person whose name they drew rather than seventeen for everyone. When Christmas came, all complied except one.

"Grandmother was the one who bought for everyone! She admitted that she worried that her grandchildren wouldn't love her if she didn't. The result was that once again she spent more than she could afford, and then she complained about it afterward," said Greta. "She made me realize that I was doing the same thing. My husband has a lot of steprelatives and I felt guilty if I didn't buy presents for them. Now I realize it's okay to say. 'I'm not willing to do that.' It's my decision and that's that."

The "I'm Not Willing" Technique will help you if you lack self-esteem, self-confidence, and problem-solving skills. It is an alternative method of making a decision about an emotional situation that could cause you to feel guilty. For instance, when you are worrying, "What will people think if I wear my skirts too short, or don't visit my parents every week, or don't retain custody of my children?" your unconscious may tell you, "If you don't do things the way people think you should, you're bad." The plain facts are, however, that you don't have to listen to this inner critic telling you that you *should* or *ought to* do a lot of things you really don't want to do. It is your decision to make and no one else's. If someone disapproves of you because of the decisions you make, it is okay; you don't have to please the entire world. You will worry a lot less when you start using the "I'm Not Willing" Technique.

Right now, write down in your journal any worries you have about what people will think. Write down exactly what your inner critic is saying you should or ought to do if you don't want to be a bad girl. Leave some space beside each incident and write in "I'm not willing to _____." Then affirm that it is perfectly acceptable for you to have your own opinions.

CHALLENGING THE "WHAT IFS?"

When Bob had agoraphobia, he did a lot of "What If?" thinking. "I would be standing in the checkout line at the supermarket telling myself, 'What if I have a panic attack and pass out and make a fool of myself?,' or I'd be driving a car and think, 'What if all of a sudden an oncoming car pulled into my lane and I had a head-on collision?' "

You don't have to be agoraphobic to engage in this kind of self-destructive thinking. Since "What If?" thinking stems from a poor self-image, women are particularly subject to it. We know college-age women who tell themselves, "What if I go to the party and no one talks to me?" and picture themselves being so disgraced and so unpopular that they will lose friends or be avoided. We know career women who ask themselves, "What if I start crying the next time that abusive supervisor screams at me?" and see themselves as being fired for doing so. We know mothers who think, "What if my son fails math?" and envision him as an adult who will never amount to anything.

"What If?" thinking creates catastrophic scenarios which make your stomach turn, your hands sweat, and your composure fail. It doesn't have to be that way. You can use our "So What?" Technique and overcome the lack of self-esteem, confidence, and problem-solving skills that generate "What If?" thinking. Every time you hear yourself thinking "What If?" simply replace it with "So what!" Look at your feelings, affirm that you are a worthy person, and think of an alternative positive outcome rather than a catastrophe.

The first time you use this technique, write it down on paper. It might read like this:

"So what if no one speaks to me at the party?"
"I would feel humiliated."
"So what?"
"I don't like to feel humiliated."
"So what?"
"So I'll find an alternative. I am a person with ideas that are interesting to others, so I can initiate some conversation myself or leave the party and find other friends who are more compatible."

Let's say you are the woman who is afraid she will cry at work:

"So what if I can't keep from crying in front of everyone?"
"I'll make a fool of myself."
"So what?"
"Other people will talk about me."
"So what?"
"They'll know I'm not perfect."
"So what?"
"I don't like not being perfect, but no one else is, either. I put up with others' imperfections, so they can put up with mine."

And the woman whose son is failing math can say:

"So what?"
"He could turn out to be a bum, and his life will be ruined."
"So what?"
"I would feel like a failure as a mother."
"So what?"
"So it means I'm not perfect, and neither is he."
"So what?"
"So I'll do the best I can to help him help himself. We'll get a tutor, and if that doesn't work, he and I will look for another solution."

The key to making the "So What?" Technique work is to keep doing it until you get down to the rock-bottom feelings that are fueling your worry, then affirm that you are OK and worthy of good things no matter what. When you become adept at challenging the "What ifs?" with "So what?," you may no longer need to write everything down.

Brainstorming, Three-D Time-Management, "I'm Not Willing," and Challenging the "What Ifs?" are three altering techniques that help you use the Second SKILL Tool to become solution-oriented rather than problem-oriented. Now we will look at finding alternatives to worry through using avoiding techniques.

GIVING UP WORRY PARTNERS

A woman with whom we worked told us that she had a "worry partner" whom she telephoned whenever she felt anxious. "We call each other and worry all the time," she said. Bob asked if the conversations helped solve any of her problems.

"No," she replied, "but it makes me feel better to know that she is worried too."

Our definition of a worry partner is someone who helps you wallow in your worry. Rather than help you seek solutions to your problem, a worry partner contributes to your feeling of being overwhelmed with negative thinking and "poor me" passivity. This is a strong behavior reinforcement. Your worry partner makes you feel good in the short term because she agrees with your outlook, so you feel okay about worrying. In our opinion, a worry partner is about as helpful as a drinking buddy. We strongly urge you to avoid being around people who keep the negative cycle going.

Bob remembers that when he moved to Midland, Texas, at the age of nine, he had a poor self-image because of his club foot. He didn't have much interest in developing friendships with the boys who were achievers, positive thinkers, and goal setters. Because of his poor self-image he shied away from them and played with the ne'er-do-wells.

"When we have a poor self-image, we attract people who demand less than the best of us," Bob says. "When I was a child, I often played the 'ain't it awful?' game with schoolmates. 'Look at all this homework. Ain't it awful that our teacher is such a jerk?' someone would say, and I'd reply, 'Yeah, school is a drag. It's just too awful. Let's skip.' When I had agoraphobia I found the same kind of friends. 'I don't know what the world is coming to these days,' I'd say. 'The politicians are money-grabbers, the streets are overrun with crooks, and the newspapers are filled with stories of murderers.' My worry partners would reinforce my negative thinking by telling horror stories of their own."

Jane admits that before her divorce, she too had a lot of worry partners. Each tried to top the other with stories about how bad his or her marriage was. Now she has a new circle of friends who are more positive and who help her stay solution-oriented.

If you worry a lot, listen to what your friends are saying to you. Are they being cheerleaders for you, building you up, and helping you find solutions? Or can they be classified as worry partners? Are they helping you sustain and maintain your worries? Take an honest look, because they may be reinforcing your worries. You may need to seek out some new friends.

How do you avoid worry partners who are members of your family? Tell them you are trying to overcome your worries. Ask them to confront you when you start to worry. Tell them to remind you of good things that have happened. If they continue to function as worry partners you may need to use distraction, the next technique.

DISTRACTING YOURSELF FROM YOUR WORRIES

Giselle had a worry that she couldn't shake. Her husband Paul had begun working late every night. When she asked why he was working late so often, Paul looked annoyed and told her that his boss had asked him to. He refused to discuss the matter. As the overtime continued, Giselle became angry at Paul's refusal to talk. She was frightened too. What if he was being secretive because he was having an affair? When Giselle discussed her feelings with a counselor, however, she realized that she had not communicated her feelings to Paul at all. When she told Paul she was angry about his silence and that his actions made her think that he was having an affair, Paul told her that his company was going through a shake-up. He felt he had to work late or lose his job. He had tried to keep his problems to himself because he had not wanted to worry her. Paul felt that the emergency situation would blow over eventually, but needed to keep on working overtime and hold on until all was well.

Giselle was convinced that Paul was telling the truth. Now, however, she worried about the effect the long hours were having on Paul's health, as well as the possibility that he would lose his job. At this point, the counselor told Giselle to try a distracting technique. "If you focus your energy on something outside your-self which is fun for you and requires your concentration, you won't worry so much about Paul," she told her.

Giselle sat down with a paper and pencil and brainstormed about what she would like to do during the evenings while Paul was away. Because she had small children, she decided to take up a hobby that she could do at home. As a teenager she had learned a little about working with stained glass. Now she had the time to develop that interest. She began to create lovely pieces of art which she could be proud of. Her worry about Paul diminished.

You can use distraction on yourself and others. Use it when family members are worry partners. If your husband responds to your worries with his own "war stories," tell him you are committed to stopping worry and that he can help you by encouraging you to think positively. Suggest that each of you sit down and write out ten positive characteristics of the other and then share them. If he continues to be negative, distract him by changing the subject. Remind him of the good things that have happened to him. By reaching out to him, you will distract yourself from your worries too.

One evening while we were sitting in the hot tub together, Jane told Bob, "I'm feeling a little sad." Bob facetiously agreed that she looked blue. Then he reminded her, "You're healthy, pretty, prosperous, and you have lots of loving friends and family, a beautiful home, a bright future, a loving marriage, and a strong spiritual life." By the time he was finished, the blue mood was gone and she was refocused on blessings, not lacks.

HANGING UP ON MR. NEGATIVE

When Bob had agoraphobia, he discovered that his negative thinking generated a lot of "What ifs?" and "What will people think?" worries which increased his stress and led to panic attacks. Because of his low self-esteem he constantly told himself that he was inferior to others and therefore unlovable. He couldn't achieve anything he set out to do. It was as if "Mr. Negative" lived inside of him, and was forever telling Bob that he was a total failure.

To develop a more positive mental attitude, Bob developed his "Hanging Up on Mr. Negative" Technique. Here is how it works: Put a rubber band around your wrist. Whenever you hear yourself saying "I can't do things as well as others," or "I'm a failure if I'm not perfect," or whenever you find yourself thinking how stupid you are and how insurmountable a problem is, simply snap the rubber band, and tell yourself, "Cancel, cancel." Then replace your negative statement with an affirmation such as, "I am a worthy person and it is perfectly all right for me to make mistakes," "I deserve love," or "Even though I have been disappointed about some things that have happened today, I can do something to make tomorrow better."

When you use this technique it is if you are refusing to answer the phone whenever Mr. Negative calls. Eventually Mr. Negative will tire of calling you, and you will have a positive, more powerful mental attitude.

Eliminating worry partners, using distraction, and "Hanging Up on Mr. Negative" are three alternatives for avoiding worry. We'll now look at some techniques that will help you make the best of accepting worries.

LEANING INTO TROUBLES

Perhaps you have a chronic illness, or you have a teenager who is barely making it through school. You use every altering and avoiding technique you can think of, but you still have the illness or your teenager still won't study. You are right to be concerned about these problems. Yet it is never good to be on the worry-go-round.

That is why we suggest you learn how to *lean in to troubles*. It involves changing your attitude toward worry so that it does not affect you so much. When you are in a fast-moving stream of worry, you have two choices: You can battle your way against the current, exhaust yourself, and find yourself being washed right back into your original position; or you can let go and see where the stream takes you. We think the second choice is better. When you let go, it sometimes takes you to a better place.

Our definition of leaning into trouble is acknowledging the power of the problem you are facing and then taking the assertive action of *not* bracing yourself against it or trying to meet it head-on. Instead you lean *into* it rather than against it. It is like letting a strong wind carry you where it will instead of standing your ground and struggling against a force that almost certainly will overpower you.

You can see the wisdom of leaning into troubles when you consider what happens in panic attacks. The more you resist them, the more you fear having them; the more you ask yourself, "What if I have one?" and conjure up worry fantasies, the more panic attacks you will have. In contrast, the more you *lean into* panic attacks by carefully noting all of your feelings (rather than bracing against them) and by telling yourself that they are not going to harm you and that the fear will diminish of its own accord—the faster you start to improve.

We want to emphasize that leaning into troubles does not mean sticking your head in the sand and telling others, "Okay, do whatever you want to me," while you keep on listening to your inner critic put you down. Leaning into your troubles should not be a form of self-punishment. It requires being assertive about your self-worth, taking action, and learning skills to survive.

"Go with it," Bob tells people who have panic attacks. "Start leaving your home. Trust that you will be okay even if a panic attack hits you in public. Let it be and in a short time the fear symptoms will go away. Each time you ride out a panic attack without resisting it, you help desensitize your body to the sensations of panic."

We can't help but admire people we have known who were dying of cancer or AIDS yet who were able to enjoy the positives in each day left to them. We call this "attitudinal healing." Rather than battling their fate, they went with it, and in some cases, their bodies reacted positively too.

Attitudinal healing sometimes turns around bad marriages and tames straying teenagers; at other times it doesn't. It simply keeps you from killing yourself with worry. We believe that this is an alternative well worth considering.

Acceptance, rather than resistance to problems, may be an entirely new concept for you. It involves determining when you have no control over others or worrisome events, letting go of unrealistic expectations for yourself and others, and living in the present moment rather than in the future or the past. Consider it as an alternative when you've done the best you can and you are still worrying.

One quick way to start letting go is to relax in a chair, then clench your hands into fists as tightly as you can. Hold them that way for a few moments, then unclench them and say, "Let go." You will feel tension draining out of your body. We'll show you more about how to heal your attitudes when you read about the Fifth SKILL Tool in chapter 10.

Once you have mastered the Second SKILL Tool, you no longer have to be a worrier, even if you have been one all your life. You now know that you have alternatives. You have the "Triple A" Formula to help you alter, avoid, or accept your worries. You may now think of yourself as a "recovering worrier." In the next chapter we will show you how the Third SKILL Tool will help you take action on those alternatives.

CHAPTER 8

◆ ◆ ◆

The Third SKILL Tool:
Image Your Goals

If you are a worrier, congratulations! You don't have to learn how to use our Third SKILL Tool. You are already a master at imaging your goals and achieving them. Why do we say that? Because the word *goals* can apply to negative as well as positive aims. Webster's Dictionary defines a goal as "the end toward which effort is directed: aim." When you worry, your *conscious* mind may be trying to prevent bad things from happening to you, but your *unconscious* mind hears only your fear. It directs its efforts to reach what it thinks is the goal: reacting to fear with panic and blocking actions that would bring about positive change. If you are a worrier, you are good at visualizing exactly what you *don't* want to have happen; you then take actions that will reap negative results. These lead to more hard luck and worry, which in turn may cause your body to succumb to stress-related illnesses like headaches, a nervous stomach, or colitis.

You can use your imaging talents to achieve positive goals. Our Third SKILL Tool provides techniques for visualizing exactly what you *do* want to have happen. We will show you how imaging good things unleashes the power of your unconscious mind to free you from worry, protect you from psychosomatic illnesses, and in many cases turn your luck around.

94

♦ *The Third SKILL Tool: Image Your Goals.*

In order to use this tool, you must first understand how your unconscious mind works.

THE BOSS NO ONE EVER TOLD YOU ABOUT

When Bob was suffering from agoraphobia, he didn't know that he had a "boss." He thought that he was in control of his life, his relationships with other people, and his thoughts. His panic disorder proved him wrong. He had a boss inside of him that directed his body to have an anxiety attack, whether or not he wanted to have it. That boss was his own unconscious mind. You have one too. Your boss can make you worry whether or not you want to.

Here is how the unconscious works: While you are going about your daily business using your logical, conscious mind, the unconscious is storing up information that it gleans from your emotions, from the way you talk to yourself, from the mental pictures you paint, and from your body language. Logic doesn't count with the unconscious. It can't tell the difference between reality and what you imagine. And whenever there is any conflict between the two minds, the unconscious always wins.

Let's say that with your conscious mind, you are thinking, "I want to be a financial success." At the same time, fear grips you when the latest batch of bills arrives in the mail. "How am I going to pay them?" you ask yourself, and your whole body becomes tense. "I'll never get out of debt. I'm a complete failure with money." In a panic, you see yourself standing on the curb sobbing while the movers carry out your furniture because the bank has foreclosed on your house and you have nowhere to live. Does your unconscious receive the message that you want to be financially successful? Not at all. Its antenna picks up your tension, your negative self-talk and the bankruptcy scenario. "Aha," says the unconscious. "This person is telling me she *wants* to be a financial failure. I'll help her reach her goal." Then it goes to work to reinforce this "reality" with a vengeance, sending back feelings of fear, failure, and poor self-esteem. When you are plagued by these feelings, you can't act appropriately to the situation; you end up reacting to your disaster fantasy instead. This sends your unconscious more signals that you are failing, and you sink deeper into the worry cycle.

In our focus groups, several women whose ex-husbands had been emotionally or physically abusive worried that they would attract future mates with the same emotional problems. "I'm a loser when it comes to men," one woman said. The only way she could picture herself with a husband was to see herself feeling fearful and resentful. Another, who had been married three times, said, "I keep myself from worrying by telling myself that I can always get a divorce if things don't work out." She saw herself as being completely unable to solve conflicts; problems could only end in divorce. These women did not realize that by picturing themselves as "losers," they were ordering their unconscious to seek out another unhappy liaison; a healthy relationship just never felt right to them.

That is the bad news—worry brings more worry. The good news is that these women can use the very same techniques that help them worry so effectively to reprogram their boss to bring them peace of mind and success. All they have to do is flip the thoughts from negative to positive.

Dr. Paul Silver, a faculty psychologist at the University of Texas Southwestern Medical Center at Dallas, uses such techniques in a treatment program for migraine sufferers which has a 70 percent to 80 percent success rate. He teaches how to restructure the way patients think about events in their lives along with visualization and relaxation.

"We tend to personalize, to misconstrue events in our lives and see them as overwhelming. When we react to our interpretations of these events, stress is increased, and this can set us up for headaches," he said. To combat the cognitive factors in migraines, he teaches patients to analyze situations so that they can expect a more realistic outcome instead of one that creates worry. To effect a physical response, he teaches progressive muscle relaxation and asks patients to visualize themselves in a relaxing place. By thinking realistically and relaxing their bodies, patients cause their arteries and veins to dilate by activating the parasympathetic branch of the autonomic nervous system. Blood flow to the body's extremities increases and the temperature in the hands and feet goes up. This alters the physiological migraine response. These same techniques, Silver believes, can be used by people hoping to overcome ordinary worry.

Here is how you can flip your worry practices from negative to positive:

- Believe with all your heart that you can change.
- Brainstorm ideas about how you can bring about good change in your life.
- Write down goals using positive language.
- Relax your body completely and visualize a happy outcome rather than a disaster.
- Affirm that you are *already* calm and free of worry.
- Take action to bring about change.
- Act as if you are carefree.

If you do these things with joyful expectation, you will be imaging success. Your internal boss will get the message and help bring about these conditions in your life, rather than block them with more worry.

Jane used the Third SKILL Tool after her divorce. Determined to find a husband with whom she would be compatible, she sat down with a pencil and piece of paper and brainstormed thirty-two qualities that she wanted in a man. From knowing how to communicate feelings to loving the ballet, each requirement was recorded. Her goal was this: "I am going to attract a man who has these thirty-two qualities." Her friends laughed and told her that she was being impossible, but Jane shrugged off their negative comments. After all, what did it hurt to make her list? Jane set aside time to relax and visualize her dream man. She affirmed that such a man was coming into her life. At the same time, she worked on herself to increase her own self-esteem so that she would be attractive to such a man. She went to places where she might meet him. When she fell in love with Bob, she found to her amazement that he had thirty of the thirty-two qualities!

"By now, he is up to thirty-one," Jane laughs. "I took him to see *Cats*, and he discovered that he really did like ballet."

If Jane had spent her time worrying that she "might make another mistake," or that "there just aren't any good men out there to marry," rather than visualizing and affirming positive thoughts and working to change herself, she believes that she would have attracted a man with few of those qualities. At the very least, she might have been so busy being negatively focused that she would have missed many golden opportunities to meet wonderful men.

"I believe that there is a law of attraction and repulsion. People who see their lives in terms of negativity, fear, and worry will attract the same kinds of people. Those who are 'into the flow of life' and expect good things to happen to them attract positive people. Women who are fearful about attracting the wrong men aren't noticing the confident and supportive men around them. When I worked on myself to become positive and self-confident, I was no longer attracted to negative men, and at the same time a loving and supportive man became attracted to me," she said.

HOW BOB LEARNED TO IMAGE POSITIVE GOALS

After Bob recovered from agoraphobia and founded Life Plus, he wanted to tell others how they could do the same thing. Bob knew, however, that he felt nervous and afraid when he had to face an audience, and he couldn't write well enough to record his experiences. Why, he was even a lousy speller! Bob could have told himself, "I'm too nervous to be a public speaker," and "I could never write a book." Instead, he wrote down his goals to do both. He made the conscious choice of believing that he could achieve his goals. Next, he learned to relax his body and visualize himself speaking before huge audiences holding a book with his name on it. He affirmed that he was a successful speaker and author. He reinforced these goals by taking action: He joined Toastmasters International to improve his speaking skills. Every week he had the opportunity to speak before supportive friends who applauded and encouraged him. He lost his fear of public speaking and began to lead workshops on stress management.

At Toastmasters, he also met writer Pauline Neff and together they decided to write his first book, *Anxiety and Panic Attacks*. Soon he was speaking on national television shows, before large conventions, and for Fortune 500 companies.

"Because I believed and expected that I would be a speaker and author and then took action, I was alert to opportunities that supported those goals. I enlisted Pauline to help me write the book. And with practice I developed the self-confidence to become a successful speaker," Bob says.

Bob says that imaging goals in a positive manner is like sailing a boat successfully. Nothing much happens when you sit on the lake at anchor. To start moving you have to act: You have to pull up your anchor and hoist your sails to catch the wind. Once you are moving, you have to adjust the sails to steer the boat. You also have to accommodate changes in the current and wind so that the boat goes where you want it to go.

You can start sailing toward your goals by pulling up the anchor of negativity and brainstorming positive results. You can adjust your visualizations and affirmations and catch the amazing power of the unconscious to bring about change. You can steer your unconscious by taking actions and opportunities that reinforce your desire to change. When you make all these changes, you will glide smoothly across your lake. What a wonderful thrill to be at the helm of your boat!

GOAL SETTING IS BELIEVING

The easiest way to stop worrying about a problem is to solve it. Because of the way your unconscious works, however, a first step to solving a problem is to quit worrying about it. If this sounds like an impossibility, remember that *feelings follow thoughts*. If you think about failure, dire consequences, and catastrophes, you will feel fear, anxiety, depression, and unhappiness. If you tell yourself that you are happy and confident because your problem is already solved, you will get off the worry-go-round. You will have your energy freed to solve the problem rather than stew about it.

Abraham Lincoln said, "Most people are as happy as they make up their minds to be." Like that great president, we are saying that you can *choose to believe* that you can be happy. When you make that choice, you have a better chance at solving your problems.

The first step is to brainstorm positive goals. Use the techniques we showed you in chapter 7. On a page in your journal, label columns with the categories of health, relationships, careers, family, finances, spiritual goals, and self-improvement. Let yourself dream about the way you would like your life to be in each category *if nothing whatsoever stood in your way.* Be extravagant! If you want a million dollars, write it down. Remember, brainstorming asks you to suspend self-judgment.

Now look at these alternatives and select one or two that you want to make your goals. Designate a section of your journal for goals and write them down. Why? As a teacher, Jane knows that you reinforce information better by using the auditory, visual, and kinesthetic (touch and movement) senses. When you write, you *feel* your fingers holding the moving pencil. You *see* the message on paper and you *hear* yourself saying it to yourself as you write it.

A famous long-term study of the success of Yale University graduates proves the importance of writing down goals. Members of a graduating class were asked how many had written down their goals for what they wanted to achieve in life. Only 3 percent had. Forty years later, these 3 percent were the top achievers of the class. The 10 percent who had had goals in mind were at the next level of success, with the rest behind.

In order to program your unconscious, write your goals in the present tense (as if you have already achieved them) and use positive language. For instance, let's say that you are worried about being able to pay the bills. You want to get off the worry-go-round and you would also like to be solvent. *Do not* word your goal this way: "I never want to worry about not having enough money again." Your unconscious hears the negatives ("never" and "not") and focuses on them—just as you used to be irresistibly tempted to do the precise thing your parents forbade you to do. Instead, write a positive goal. Phrase it in the present tense: "I have (right now) an abundant supply of resources to meet all my obligations in a free and easy manner." When your unconscious hears present-tense thinking, it believes that your goal is already true. It assumes that this is a normal and achievable state for you, and it goes to work to relax you and open you to getting what you want.

Write each goal on a separate page, date it, and record exactly what you will do to achieve your goal. For instance, after stating your goal of having abundant resources, list actions you can take to make that happen:

1. Three times a day I will relax and visualize myself having plenty of money.
2. I will brainstorm ways to increase my money supply.
3. I will choose the best ones to work on.

Suppose you choose to take a course that will enable you to earn more money. Write another goal sheet that states: "I am completing my course in _____. Then list steps such as:

1. I will telephone the school and register for the course.
2. I will buy the supplies I need for the course.
3. I will rearrange my work schedule so that I can attend the course.
4. I will relax each day and see myself enjoying the class.

Always leave space for writing in "achieved" when your goal is accomplished.

RELAXATION—THE KEY TO CONTACTING YOUR BOSS

Once you have written out a detailed plan of what you will do to achieve your goal, the next step is to create some affirmations and visualizations about yourself. An affirmation is simply a positive statement about yourself indicating your inherent worth or your abilities. As an example, you might write, "I am a worthy person who deserves love," "I am perfectly capable of passing a course that will help me make more money," or "I am good at math." A visualization is a mental image of yourself doing the very thing that you want to happen. The visualizations that correlate with these affirmations might include seeing yourself with your husband in a loving moment, seeing yourself sitting in a classroom with a smile on your face, or handing in a financial report and being congratulated by your boss.

Underneath your goal, write down the subheadings "Affirmations" and "Visualizations" and briefly note some of them. Leave space for recording whether or not you have used them every day. You can program your unconscious to make the positive changes you desire by affirming yourself and visualizing while relaxing your body so completely that your brain waves actually cycle at a lower rate.

Your affirmations and visualizations will be effective only if you use them while in the relaxed state which is called "alpha." At this level, your brain waves cycle at the rate of seven to fourteen cycles per minute. The alpha state is the perfectly natural state you are in when you first wake up in the morning or right before you fall asleep. It is the quiet, intuitive, creative state when your unconscious can hear your commands. Practitioners of meditation, certain yoga techniques, and contemplative prayer also attain the alpha state. While you are in alpha, you feel awake and alert, yet your thinking is dominated by the right brain, which processes images and detects patterns.

In *Anxiety and Panic Attacks* and *Beyond Fear*, Bob provides detailed scripts for readers to tape and play back in order to undergo a progressive relaxation of all the muscles of the body. But you don't have to have a tape to relax. Simply find a quiet place where you will be undisturbed, close your eyes, and command your body to release tension in every part. For instance, after making a fist and holding your hands clenched for three or four seconds, completely relax the tension and tell yourself, "My hands are as limp as those of a rag doll." Release tension in all parts of your body, including your head and face, in the same way.

Not only is the alpha state the most effective way of reprogramming your boss, but by learning to relax you give your body time off from the physical effects of anxiety. When you are feeling tense and nervous, you can put yourself in alpha and feel relief. It is also a great way to combat insomnia.

To reprogram your unconscious, use your visualizations and affirmations while you are in alpha. If you are a worrier, you already know how to visualize. You daydream about the horrors of approaching your manager for a raise and being turned down, or falling on your face when you go to the microphone to make your speech. You fantasize that your husband is having a drink with the pretty new colleague in his office while your stomach churns with fear.

All you have to do to change these worry scenarios into positive visualizations is to change the ending to a happy one. See your boss telling you that he has noticed how competent you are and that he is putting in a requisition for a raise. Picture yourself with a smile on your face as you end your speech and listen to the audience applaud. See your husband looking lovingly at you while the pretty colleague walks away in the background.

Don't wait until you are in alpha to create visualizations and affirmations. *Write them down in advance in your journal.* Make them positive and use all five senses when you are describing your fantasies. Smell and feel the leather upholstery in the boss' office. Taste the coffee he offers you. Paint the walls of the meeting room where you make your speech in bright, joyous colors. Hear the enthusiastic applause. See your goals as already met: You have the agreeable boss, the interesting speech, or attentive husband *right now.* If you use "someday," "in the future," or "I don't want to be," or "I wish," your unconscious will hear only uncertainty and go to work to perpetuate your worries and your problems.

Be sure to frame your affirmations positively and in the present tense, as you did with your goals. Write down, for example, "I am deserving of a raise and my manager knows that," "I make interesting speeches that people like to hear," or "I am attractive to my husband."

Then relax and visualize and affirm yourself as being *already free of your worry or problem.* For instance, if you want to be able to pay the bills, visualize yourself sitting at your desk writing checks and noting that the balance in your checkbook is high. See yourself taking care of this paperwork confidently, with a happy smile on your face. Create other visualizations in which you see yourself enjoying your financial security. Perhaps you have bought yourself a beautiful new dress or a sparkly piece of jewelry and still have money left over. While you are visualizing, use the affirmation you have written down in advance, such as, "I have all the resources I need to take care of any obligations I might incur and still have money left over."

You might "anchor in" the calm feelings as is done in neuro-linguistic programming by asking a friend to touch you gently but firmly on the forearm while you are visualizing. Then whenever you are worrying, you only have to touch yourself in the same place to recall the worry-free feeling.

The more frequently you program your unconscious in this way, the sooner your boss will get the message and make change easier for you. For daily worries, use these relaxation and programming techniques in the morning when you first wake up and also in the evening before going to bed. If your worry level is breaking all records, go to alpha several times a day—in the morning when you first wake up, at midmorning, after lunch, at midafternoon, after supper, and at bedtime. When Bob was using the Third SKILL Tool to overcome the negativity and worry that accompanied his agoraphobia, he used this technique six times a day.

ACTION AND HOW TO MAKE IT HAPPEN

Once you have caught the power of the unconscious in your sails, you must steer your sailboat where you want to go. That means creating an action plan that outlines the specific steps you will take to help you reach your goal. Brainstorm for ideas and write down everything that comes to mind, no matter how outrageous. Make a navigation map!

"Many people just sit around waiting for good things to happen and worry when they don't," Jane says. "I have a friend who for seven years has refused even to unpack her decorative accessories because she is waiting until she has all the money she needs to completely redecorate her whole house. She won't do anything to make her home look better. The result is that she is ashamed to invite anyone over. Even if she doesn't have money for a complete redecorating job, she could refinish a table or buy curtains or a picture that she loves. She could unpack her favorite items to make the atmosphere homey and comfortable and stop worrying about and waiting for perfection."

Here are some alternatives you might brainstorm to meet the goal of being able to pay your bills: You might make more sales calls, go after a raise at work, take a second job, change careers, or sell something you own. You might supplement your income by tutoring if you are a teacher or by working overtime.

When you have selected one or two actions you will take to make yourself financially secure, write them down on your goal sheet under a subheading titled "Action." It is easier to progress in small steps rather than in giant steps, so consider such actions as cutting up your credit card or brown-bagging lunch for a month rather than planning to change jobs within the month. Leave space beside each action so that you can check off your success. Working on action steps and checking off each accomplishment is a great way to overcome the lack of confidence that so many women have. Each time you succeed, no matter how small the challenge, and *acknowledge that success*, you build your self-esteem.

CONTACTING YOUR BOSS BY ACTING *AS IF*

Another kind of action you can take to stop worrying is to act *as if* what you want to happen has already happened. To stop worrying about whether you are liked at the office, act *as if* you are liked and reach out to others. To stop worrying about whether you can pay the bills, wear your nicest outfit and look *as if* you are affluent.

If you think we are asking you to fake it, we are! But the faking only lasts for a little while, as you will discover. How does faking work? Acting *as if* is to behavior what positive words are to thinking. By faking your feelings and actions for a time, you inform your unconscious that you are already the way you want to be. Your boss gets the message and helps you achieve your goal.

When Bob wanted to become a public speaker, he acted *as if* he were a pro every time he gave a speech at Toastmasters meetings. Even though his knees shook, he acted as confidently as he could. (By relaxing, visualizing, and affirming that he was enjoying his speech ahead of time, his unconscious helped him to feel more calm.) Each completed speech was a reinforcing message to his boss that he could do it—and even like it. Eventually his unconscious understood: "Public speaking is great!" Then he no longer felt afraid. Now he makes a career of speaking to thousands of people each year.

Write your *acting as ifs* on your goal sheet. For instance, if you want to be liked at the office write:

* Every day I will smile and say hello to everyone I meet in the hall.
* Every day I will give a compliment to three people.

Leave space beside each *acting as if* goal. Check them off daily to be sure that you do them.

GOAL SHEETS FOR INCREASING SELF-ESTEEM

Many women tell us they worry about their children's health, grades, associations with negative friends, bad habits, and just about everything else. They don't realize that by allowing these problems to put them on the worry-go-round, they model negative behavior. Their children become timid and lack self-confidence because that is the parental model they see for dealing with life's challenges.

You can't program your unconscious to "fix" your children or your husband or your co-workers, but you can image a goal *for yourself* to become more confident and skilled at dealing with problems that concern your children. When you use the techniques of the Third SKILL Tool, your unconscious will see to it that you act in confident ways. You'll find that others will react as well.

Here are some sample goal sheets for increasing your self-esteem as you deal with the three areas most vital to women: family, work, and love.

Situation: You have a fourteen-year-old son whom you have informed that it is time he washed his own clothes. When he doesn't do it, you rescue him by washing his clothes for him, yet you feel angry and resentful. "There must be something wrong with me, because he's not being fair to me," you tell yourself. A counselor tells you the solution is to let him dress in dirty clothes until he decides to wash them himself, but a voice in your head says, "What will people think about me if he wears dirty clothes?"

Here is how you might create a goal sheet to do what you must and not worry about it:

Goal: I nurture myself and feel perfectly calm when my son refuses to wash his clothes.

GOAL SHEET #1

Techniques	*Daily Checkoff*						
	Su	M	Tu	W	Th	F	Sa

Visualizations

1. I see myself looking at my son in a calm, detached manner whenever I see him in dirty clothing.

2. My body is perfectly relaxed while I see myself telling my son that I want him to wash his clothes.

3. I see myself giving myself a tiara, scepter, and a banner to wear across my chest that reads "Good Mother."

Affirmations

1. I am a person of worth who is doing her son a favor by standing firm.

2. I am perfectly confident and within my rights to demand that my son wash his own clothes.

3. I love myself and that is good.

Actions

1. I will write out affirmative ways to communicate with my son.

2. I will reward myself by taking a bubble bath or reading another chapter in my favorite book every time I communicate affirmatively with my son.

3. I will read over my goal sheet every day and use the techniques.

Techniques	Daily Checkoff						
	Su	M	Tu	W	Th	F	Sa

Acting As If
1. When I am with my son, I will act as if I do not notice that he is wearing dirty clothes.

2. If others comment on my son's condition, I will smile and tell them that I am proud of myself for letting him take responsibility for himself.

3. If my son complains about his dirty clothes, I will smile and say, "Yes, they are dirty, aren't they," while I mentally pat myself on the back.

Situation: You have a co-worker who frequently criticizes or undercuts you. Because you have a habit of worrying about what other people think, you feel angry and depressed whenever you are around him. You recognize that your self-esteem plummets every time he speaks out, yet you can't avoid him. You start stumbling over words and feeling ridiculous each time you must deal with him. Here is how you might make a goal sheet to change this situation. Work on yourself and see if the new you does not change your co-worker too.

Goal: I feel so good about myself that I am free of worry about what _____ (the criticizer) thinks of me.

GOAL SHEET #2

Techniques	Daily Check-off						
	Su	M	Tu	W	Th	F	Sa

Visualizations
1. I see myself with a smile on my face whenever I am with _____.

2. I see myself receiving a report card marked "excellent" in the category "self-worth."

Techniques	Daily Check-off
	Su M Tu W Th F Sa

3. I see myself speaking to _____ in a calm, controlled manner, telling him that I don't like what he says and asking him to refrain from criticism. I see him smiling in return.

4. I see myself speaking calmly when _____ is around; my body is relaxed and my thoughts are clear.

Affirmations

1. I am a lovely, kind, happy, confident, and competent person who deserves success.

2. I feel perfectly calm whenever I am with _____.

3. It is perfectly all right for me to stand up for myself.

Actions

1. I will learn how to relax so that I can use my visualizations and affirmations.

2. I will read a book on how to be more assertive.

3. I will read over my goal sheet every day and use the techniques.

Acting As If

1. When I am with _____, I will smile a lot.

2. I will join a support group that will help me develop confidence. I will be aware of my confident demeanor when doing other tasks that I enjoy.

3. I will listen to _____'s complaints and then tell him my feelings clearly and professionally.

Situation: Your husband frequently puts you down. Here is how you might word a goal sheet to deal with that situation:

Goal: I feel good about myself whenever I confront my husband for putting me down.

GOAL SHEET #3

Techniques	*Daily Checkoff*						
	Su	M	Tu	W	Th	F	Sa

Visualizations

1. I see myself looking calm and unruffled as I tell my husband, "I will not accept being put down by you."

2. I see myself smiling while my husband apologizes for putting me down.

3. I see "You're stupid" printed on yellow balloons which float away in the sky.

Affirmations

1. I am a perfectly confident, intelligent woman who loves herself.

2. I feel perfectly calm whenever I confront my husband for putting me down.

3. I am perfectly free of any anger or resentment because I can prevent my husband from putting me down.

Actions

1. I will attain an alpha state every day to relax and practice confronting my husband.

2. I will sign up for an assertiveness-training class.

3. I will write down a variety of ways I can confront my husband and practice saying them out loud.

Techniques	*Daily Checkoff*						
	Su	M	Tu	W	Th	F	Sa

Acting As If

1. I will act as if none of my husband's put-downs affect me in the least.

2. I will reward myself whenever I successfully confront my husband by writing down all the good things I can think of about myself.

3. I will tell my husband that I love myself.

In the next chapter, we will explain more detailed ways of taking action to influence your unconscious and stop worrying. Those too will go on your goal sheet.

BUT DOES IT WORK?

The Wizard of Oz is a children's tale that teaches the very same lesson we're trying to explain. All the main characters had goals. The scarecrow wanted a brain, the tin man a heart, and the cowardly lion courage. Dorothy wanted to get back home. The four imaged and acted on their goals. They believed that the Wizard could give them what they wanted, so they set out on the yellow brick road and met with adventures galore. The charm of the story is that even though the scarecrow, tin man, and lion found the wizard to be a fake, they realized that they already possessed what they thought only a wizard could provide. Dorothy discovered the best gift of all: The people she had left behind were the most important part of her life because they really loved her.

The self-worth that can save you from negativity and worry are already yours too; you were born with it. All you have to do to tap into it is to acknowledge it. With our Third SKILL Tool, you can set your goal and find the wizard inside—your unconscious—that will help you claim yourself as a worthy person who deserves to be free of unnecessary worrying. When you walk down that yellow brick road, you will see others in a different light as well.

CHAPTER 9

♦ ♦ ♦

The Fourth SKILL Tool: Let Yourself Risk

Our friend Judith Briles, author of *The Confidence Factor*, says that a lot of women worry because they spend all their time saying, "One for the money, two for the show, three to get ready, three to get ready, three to get ready . . ."

In the last chapter we showed how you can use the Third SKILL Tool to enlist a very powerful ally—your unconscious—to overcome worry and solve problems. Unless you are willing to take action and work *with* your unconscious, however, you may be stuck in the broken record Judith talks about. That is why it is important to master the Fourth Tool as well.

♦ *The Fourth SKILL Tool: Let Yourself Risk.*

We have worked with many women who imaged goals to lose weight, make more money, get a better job, or stop worrying about their children. They even wrote down the steps they would take to achieve their goals. But when it came to taking those steps, their resolve faltered. Why? Because they would have to *risk* making some changes in their lives, and nobody likes a change except a wet baby! They didn't know whether they would succeed or fail, and they couldn't bear the thought of making a mistake. It was safer to stay miserable than to risk change. By not taking action, however, these women were informing their unconscious that they wanted to stay the way they were.

Jim Wilson, Bob's psychologist friend, says that six little words identify the chronic worrier. "Oh, no!," "What if?," and "Yes, but." Here is a typical conversation between Jim and a worrying client:

> CLIENT: *"Oh, no*, something terrible is going to happen."
> JIM: "The facts don't seem to indicate that."
> CLIENT: "But *what if* you're wrong?"
> JIM: "Well, aren't things going pretty well right this moment?"
> CLIENT: *"Yes, but* things can change."

When you are afraid to risk, you are saying, "I may be miserable, but at least it's a misery I am comfortable with. I don't know what I might have to face if things changed."

When a professional-speaker friend we'll call Helen asked Jane's advice on increasing her income, Jane suggested that she apply to an agency that arranges seminars and workshops. Jane told her that speakers could apply to lead either half-day or full-day programs.

"Oh, no, I could never do that," Helen said. "I'm a speaker, not a trainer or a workshop leader."

"Anyone who speaks as well as you can learn to lead a workshop," Jane said.

"But *what if* I tried to do it and I ran out of material? I've never spoken for longer than an hour," Helen protested.

"Couldn't you devise some audience participation activities that take up time and help people internalize the points you make in your speech?" Jane suggested.

"Yes, but I've never done that kind of work. I would probably be a total failure," Helen said.

"Why don't you apply, anyway?" Jane said. "A lot of speakers find the agency helpful."

"Yes, but they have more on the ball than I do. *What if* I made a fool of myself?" Helen said. *"Oh, no*, I'd better not."

Helen had the desire and the ability to progress in her career. She had set her goals, but she was not going to achieve them. By refusing to risk, Helen was succumbing to the Three Lacks which keep so many women behind. She lacked enough self-esteem that the thought of failure threatened her. Nor did she have enough self-confidence to believe in her ability to do new things. She didn't know how to solve problems and make decisions, so she did not understand how to take the steps that would help her master a new skill. All she could do was worry that she wasn't progressing in her career.

THE PROS AND CONS OF TAKING A RISK

Jane Adams, author of *Wake Up, Sleeping Beauty*, writes that everyone has two internal voices which she calls the Keeper and the Seeker. Both are necessary for emotional balance. The Keeper, which wants you to stay as you are, buffers you from change and maintains your basic identity. Even if you are disfigured in an accident, for instance, the Keeper helps you realize that you are still the same person inside that you always were. The Seeker, which calls out for change, enables you to grow and improve. Sometimes you shut out the Seeker, because change requires taking risks and accepting losses. When you risk moving to a new city, you lose old friends and familiar surroundings, but you also have the possibility of making new and exciting acquaintances.

The problem with being involved too much with the Keeper is that you never stop worrying. Until you step out and attempt a new way of thinking, behaving, responding, and reacting, you will stay on the worry-go-round. You have to be willing to feel unsettled if you try something new and make mistakes, or to lose the approval of those who may not respond when you try to reach out to them. In other words, you have to be willing to fail. Ultimately, it is the only way to overcome your tendency to worry.

Shirley Hutton reported in the May 1989 issue of *Working Woman* magazine that she took a risk by quitting an $11,000-a-year job as a television talk-show host fourteen years ago to begin a full-time career in direct sales at Mary Kay Cosmetics, Inc. By recruiting others to sell Mary Kay products, she could make profits

on their sales and the sales of those whom they recruited as well. She set a goal to call at least ten new leads each day. By her third year of selling, she had earned $60,000. She then took the risk of spending her own money to travel and meet potential recruits. She even approached strangers. Now she shares in the profits of 50,000 sales reps in the United States and Canada. She has a net worth of $3 million, brings in a steady income of $400,000 a year, and continues to recruit. How does she avoid worrying about being rejected?

"If women choose not to listen to me, I just say to myself, 'Let them go wrinkle,' " she told *Working Woman.*

When Heather listened to her Seeker, the rewards were not so clear-cut, she told us. As a partner with her husband in a small retail shop, she was elected the token woman on the board of a suburban chamber of commerce.

"At first I was so thrilled by being the only woman in my community who was honored in this way that I only sat and listened. Then I realized that the men on the board were taking some actions that I considered to be unethical. I began to speak out, but they wouldn't listen. Some were rude and told me to be quiet.

"It was embarrassing to be treated in this way. I felt terribly rejected. I was afraid that if I continued to press for what I felt was right, I would lose my position on the board. When I asked my mother if she thought that I should be quiet, she told me absolutely not. Mother was a single parent when I was growing up. She had to learn assertiveness, and she thought I needed to learn it, too. I kept on speaking out, and when my two-year term was over, I wasn't reappointed.

"You might say that I took a risk and failed, but three years later I can truthfully say that I didn't. Since then, other women have served on the board, and because I spoke up, they have too. Some wonderful changes have been accomplished that just wouldn't have happened if I had given up. I grew a lot too. I'll never again be the timid, worried woman in a man's world that I used to be."

Bob remembers how the fear of failure kept him from setting goals to change his behavior before he had agoraphobia. "I used to think that if I *made* a mistake, then I *was* a mistake, so I never set

any goals to change. I didn't understand that risking, failing, and trying again is just a process that you go through to get where you want to go. How many wrong notes did Van Cliburn strike while learning to play the piano? How many tennis balls has Steffi Graf hit into the net? It really doesn't matter. Few mistakes we make are so devastating that we can't recover from them. We worry about a lot of little things that don't matter. By not risking, we become paralyzed with fear. We get stuck in bad relationships and careers. We spend a lot of time on the worry-go-round."

Ultimately, it took a crippling problem like agoraphobia to give Bob a burning desire to change that outweighed his fear of failure. He risked setting goals to overcome his negative thinking and to improve mentally, physically, and spiritually. He took action and found Life Plus. But you needn't wait until things become disastrous to take a step toward change. You can start right now—read on!

RISKING BY BEING ASSERTIVE

Our Fourth SKILL Tool emphasizes three risking principles. Using them, you can overcome the worry thoughts that are generated by a lack of self-esteem and self-confidence. You can increase your ability to make decisions and solve problems. Let yourself risk by:

- Changing your thoughts
- Changing your words
- Changing your actions

In chapter 8 you saw that *feelings follow thoughts*. Negative thoughts program your unconscious to bring about negative feelings which in turn cause you to act in negative ways. We showed you how to convert your unconscious into a powerful ally for making positive changes. Now we want to show you the action steps you can take to reinforce this programming. As you risk using them, you will learn problem-solving skills and gain self-confidence.

The process involves learning to *discern* when you are thinking negatively and then making the conscious choice to *think, communicate,*

and *act* in positive ways. In effect, we want you to learn how to be assertive. When you risk *thinking* assertively, you will silence the inner critic that causes you to worry about mistakes or falling short of the mark. When you *communicate* assertively, you will signal your unconscious that your self-esteem is intact. Others will hear the message and respond differently too. When you *act* assertively, you solve the problems that generate anxiety. You build confidence to deal with future concerns.

We want to make it clear, however, that there is a big difference between assertive and aggressive behavior. Robert E. Alberti and Michael L. Emmons, authors of *Your Perfect Right*, point out that assertiveness is not a tool for manipulating others but for making your relationships more equal.

"Assertive behavior promotes equality in human relationships, enabling us to act in our own best interests, to stand up for ourselves without undue anxiety, to express feelings honestly and comfortably, to exercise personal rights without denying the rights of others," they say. "The person who carries a desire for self-expression to the extreme of aggressive behavior accomplishes goals at the expense of others."

The overweight wife whose husband nags and teases her for being unattractive can choose to react nonassertively, aggressively, or assertively. A nonassertive response is to ignore the comments, feel guilty about being overweight, and worry whether a divorce is in the offing. An aggressive response is to retaliate by nagging about the bad habits of her mate, such as being a lousy sex partner. An assertive response is to agree that she does need to lose weight and to point out that she is doing her best and having a hard time. She would then tell him that she does not appreciate his taunts. She would suggest ways that he might reinforce her for her efforts to lose weight so that they can both work toward the goal they want.

Before she can react rationally to his teasing, however, she may need to analyze what her inner critic is telling her. Is it telling her, "Why can't you lose weight just like everyone else does? No wonder your husband puts you down. You can't do anything right." If she listens to the critic and risks no communication with her husband, she is reacting nonassertively and setting herself up for a lot of worry.

Is she feeling so guilty and resentful at what her inner critic is telling her that she will react aggressively by lashing out at her husband? If so, she is setting herself up to become a victim of what psychologists call cognitive distortions. Her flawed perception of herself keeps her from functioning rationally. She must become aware of these distortions and learn to restructure them before she can communicate assertively.

To be assertive rather than aggressive you have to find perfect balance on the seesaw of your self-perception. If you are weighted down with poor self-esteem, you will be on the down side of the seesaw, sunk in anxiety. If you give in to resentment, you will be on the up side of the seesaw, berating others. If your self-worth is high, you will be in the middle, feeling capable of communicating rationally and solving problems. By bringing in the added weight of assertiveness, you can raise your partner's self-esteem, too. Eventually you may be perfectly balanced on the seesaw in a win-win position.

THE INNER CRITIC'S TOP TEN COGNITIVE DISTORTIONS

To become aware of your inner critic's Top Ten Cognitive Distortions, study the list below. Note how you can restructure these distortions. When you hear yourself reacting irrationally to the inner critic, write the distortion down in your journal and immediately counter it with the truth. Relax, affirm, and visualize yourself thinking in a calm, rational manner.

1. *Perfectionism* causes you to set unreasonably high standards for yourself and others. Even though you have achieved at levels society considers normal or even above par, your inner critic tells you that you are a failure or that your accomplishments are due to mere luck. Restructure your thoughts by reminding yourself that you are a person of worth regardless of your achievements. You deserve love, happiness, and self-acceptance just as you are.

2. *Rejectionitis* is exaggerating a single rejection until it dominates your thoughts. If a good-looking fellow at a party ignores you and talks to someone else, you tell yourself you're just not attrac-

tive to men. Restructure by reminding yourself that you cannot expect every man to prefer you to others. After all, you have your favorites too. You have plenty of good qualities that appeal to most people. Make a list of your good qualities and also of the men who do like you.

3. *Negative focus* obliterates all the positives in your life because you can see only one negative situation. When Jane focused on her scars as a child, she brought on low self-esteem because she didn't see all her good qualities. Restructure by making a list of your good qualities and visualizing and affirming that you are great.

4. *Refusing the positives* is telling yourself that even the good things in your life are negatives. It is reacting to a compliment on your appearance with a "Yes, but my hair is a mess and my face is all broken out." Restructure by reminding yourself that people don't pass out compliments if they don't want to. If someone compliments you, rejoice. Say "Thanks," and not another word.

5. *White-is-black thinking* is using neutral or even positive facts to draw negative conclusions. When your boyfriend is moody, you immediately start worrying that you did something to make him angry, when in reality he may be worrying about a report he needs to write at work. Restructure by reminding yourself that others are responsible for their own behavior and that you will take responsibility for your worry by communicating with him assertively, asking if something is bothering him. Another form of white-is-black thinking is to predict dire consequences for every action you want to take. Perhaps you tell yourself that if you try to be assertive with your moody boyfriend, you will make a fool out of yourself and he will be angry. Restructure by recognizing that you have no way of knowing what he will say or how the future will be. Visualize and affirm a happy outcome instead of a catastrophe.

6. *Stretch- or shrink-thinking* is either stretching the truth into an anxiety-producing scenario when you've done something that you're less than proud of or shrinking the good that you did until it is invisible. When you forget your best friend's birthday, you may stretch-think: "She'll never forgive me. I'm an inconsiderate idiot." Restructure with the reality that everyone forgets birthdays from time to time and you are still a worthy person. You can apologize and give her a belated present. On the other hand, when you

diminish the value of an award you won by telling everyone, "It's no big deal," you are shrink-thinking. Restructure by reminding yourself that it is okay to pat yourself on the back and even acknowledge yourself aloud, if you can. You are sending good messages to your unconscious, which in turn will create self-confidence that overcomes worry.

7. *Fictional fantasizing* is substituting emotions for facts. It is telling yourself that because you have an irrational fear of flying, bad things are bound to happen to you if you get on a plane. It is waking up in the morning feeling apprehensive because of a worrisome dream you can't remember and telling everyone, "I got up on the wrong side of the bed. This is going to be a bad day." Restructure by making the choice to change your distorted thoughts. The day doesn't have to be bad just because you didn't sleep well. Visualize and affirm happy, peaceful scenarios and program your unconscious to send you calm thoughts.

8. *"Should" and "ought" legalisms* are your inner critic's assertions that you are imperfect if you don't do what it tells you is the only acceptable way to do things. "I *should* be able to control my children better," or "I *ought* to be able to keep the house cleaner," are distortions that can lead to resentment and guilt. Restructure by reminding yourself that you are responsible only for your own actions, not those of your father, mother, children, or the next door neighbor. Affirm that you are a worthy person as you are.

9. *Mistaken identity* is telling yourself that you are all bad because you made a mistake. Say you had a relationship with a man who abused you, and you now tell yourself, "I'm just stupid when it comes to men, so now I'll have to pay for it." Restructure by reminding yourself that everyone makes mistakes and that you are still a person of worth. Set a goal of getting counseling to help you make a better selection in the future.

10. *"My Fault" thinking* is assuming responsibility for a negative event when the responsibility is not yours. In this case, you don't make the mistake—others do—yet you assume all the blame. If your husband drinks too much and makes a scene, you cry, "My fault," and blame yourself for "making him so miserable he had to drink." Restructure by reminding yourself that you are responsible only for your own behavior, not anyone else's.

When you are stuck on the worry-go-round, take a look at these Top Ten and see if your inner critic is causing you to distort the truth about yourself and events. If so, write down how you will restructure your thoughts, then reprogram your unconscious to think rationally.

EIGHT TIPS FOR COMMUNICATING ASSERTIVELY

The second risking principle is to *change your words*—to communicate assertively. We find that this kind of change is especially hard for women. Holly told her focus group, "When I flew home one weekend, a friend invited herself to share in the activities I had planned with my parents. Although I love my friend, I wanted to reserve time for my family alone, but I couldn't bring myself to tell her that. I was afraid that if I was honest with her, I would hurt her feelings. So I did a lot of hinting. I talked around the issue in circles and never got my message across. I was angry and resentful the whole weekend, worrying that it wasn't fair to my parents."

If Holly had handled this problem assertively, she would have told her friend, "I love being with you, but I want to reserve this weekend for my parents alone. Is there another time when we can see each other?"

Instead, Holly chose to fall into the nonassertive trap because of her distorted cognitions. She was using white-is-black thinking by predicting that her friend would be hurt when there was no way to know how the friend would react. When she pictured her friend being angry and herself feeling distressed, Holly was using the "My Fault" distortion. She was taking responsibility for her friend's feelings. Holly's nonassertive behavior is not unusual, however. Because most little girls are encouraged to be pleasers and nurturers, many women suffer in silence rather than express their feelings honestly. They don't realize that by being nonassertive, they actually compound their worries. For instance, by trying to please, Holly developed resentment toward her friend, which damaged their relationship. She also was left with the worry that she had ruined the weekend for herself and her parents.

When you disagree with others, how assertive can you be in

expressing yourself? Are you completely honest about how you feel, or do you tell yourself your feelings don't matter and set yourself up for resentment and worry? Here are some steps you can take to become a more assertive communicator:

1. *Plan to express your feelings.* Label a sheet of paper "My Feelings" and actually sit down and think about your problem. If you are a pleaser, you may have been telling yourself, "*Yes*, my husband and I have financial problems, and it seems like he shouldn't have bought that sports car considering that we're late paying the rent again this month, *but* we're working on the problem." Note that this is a variation of *yes, but.* It indicates that you are feeling fearful of making changes, but that is not all. What are you feeling about your husband's actions? Is it anger? Disappointment? Write down how you honestly feel. If you really can't tell, proceed to the next step.

2. *Describe the situation.* Divide your sheet of paper into two columns with one titled, "The Problem," and the other "My Part in the Problem." In the first column write about the situation in detail as honestly as you can. In the second column, check the list of Top Ten Cognitive Distortions and list any that apply to it. Are you thinking with "should" and "ought" legalisms that tell you that you *should* let your husband control the purse strings no matter how irresponsible he is? Are you doing white-is-black thinking and predicting dire circumstances if you ask your husband to limit his spending? Are you telling yourself "My fault," and thinking that if you had been a better wife he wouldn't have wanted to go out and spend all that money? Then write down how you will restructure your cognitions. (Note: By describing the situation in this way, you may become aware of other feelings you have about the situation. If so, write them under step 1.)

3. *Write down alternative ways of handling your problem.* You might write, "He could turn the responsibility for paying bills over to me;" "we could set up a budget and live by it;" "he could get a second job and make more money to pay for the luxuries he wants;" "we could go to a financial counselor and see about consolidating our debts."

4. *Plan how you will communicate about the problem.* Write out: "My feelings are _____. The reason that I feel this way is

because _____ (name of person involved) is _____ (write action that disturbs you). Alternatives I can suggest are _____.

For instance, you might write, "I am angry at my husband because he spent money that we don't have on a sports car. I am embarrassed and worried because we don't have money to pay the rent. Some alternatives are: we could set up a budget and we could go to a financial counselor to consolidate our debts."

5. *Practice your assertive communication.* Find a place where you can be alone and set an empty chair facing you. Now practice saying how you feel and why. Suggest your alternatives firmly.

6. *Relax, visualize, and affirm yourself communicating assertively.* See yourself speaking calmly with your husband. Tell yourself: "I am perfectly calm and capable of talking about finances to my husband."

7. *Communicate with the person involved.*

8. *Let go of the consequences.* This is a crucial point. When you communicate assertively, you will likely receive some kind of positive response; however, you might not. We have known plenty of women who mastered the steps to assertive communication who did not solve their problems: When Heather spoke out to the chamber of commerce board members, they became angry. The plain facts are that some people have yet to accept assertiveness in anyone—especially in women. You need to expect that attitude because there are going to be differences in the way people respond to you. You must keep in mind that this is a natural reaction and has nothing to do with your being good or bad.

Even if your assertive communication does not bring you the desired result, you are in any case overcoming the Three Lacks by practicing it. You will feel less worry and resentment when you express how you feel honestly. And you are setting up a new way of being that may forestall similar problems in the future.

ASSERTIVE ACTIONS

The third risking principle is to *change your actions.* You don't just sit back and wait for problems to solve themselves. You brainstorm solutions and take steps.

One psychologist told us that he had a client who was less than five feet tall who was married to a physically abusive husband twice her size. Whenever she tried to communicate assertively, he slapped her. Rather than get a divorce, she took karate lessons. One day when they were arguing, he raised his hand to slap her. Before he knew what happened, she had flipped him down on the floor! It wasn't long before the husband agreed to getting some counseling himself. Now they are on the way to having a more compatible marriage.

When you are worried about a situation, brainstorm the actions that you can take to help bring about a solution. (Refer to the brainstorming guidelines in chapter 7.) Can you take a course that will help you make more money, understand your children better, or improve your appearance? Can you join a support group, get some counseling, or read a book that will help you? Be creative. Write down the action you will take, program your unconscious to help you be successful, and then go out and do it!

HOW HILDA RISKED CHANGING

We could not help but be impressed at what a difference it made to a speaker we will call Hilda when she risked replacing aggressiveness with assertiveness in her thinking, communicating, and acting. She might never have taken those risks, however, if she had not been faced with a crisis that left her with few other alternatives.

It happened when Hilda emceed a speaker association meeting at which Abbie and Harry were scheduled to speak. When Abbie talked too long, Hilda signaled her to relinquish the floor, but Abbie wouldn't stop. She didn't realize that the clock at the back of the room had stopped running. She thought that she still had ten minutes to talk. When Hilda again gave her the cut-off sign, Abbie nodded at the clock and kept on talking. Hilda felt a lot of pressure to keep things moving because Harry had told her that he had to catch a plane after the meeting. He couldn't afford to run late.

Finally Hilda stood up and said in a loud aggressive tone, "For God's sake, Abbie, stop your talking. Harry's got to catch a plane." Abbie reacted with rage.

"That's *my* problem?" she snapped back. She then continued talking for ten more minutes! Afterward Hilda and Abbie went into the hall and started screaming insults at each other. Other members joined them. Soon everyone was taking sides. They didn't blame the clock. They blamed Hilda. They said she came on too strong—that she always came on too strong.

Hilda was hurt and angry. No one involved had much sympathy for her. After worrying about it all night, she took a big risk. The next day she came to Bob and asked him to tell her the truth.

"Everybody tells me I'm power hungry," she said. "I keep getting this feedback that I'm condescending and arrogant."

"Hilda, if everyone is telling you this, I think you have to take a look at it," Bob said. "I agree that you come across that way."

"I do?" she said, completely bewildered. "But what can I do about it?"

"If you think this kind of behavior serves you well, then continue. If you don't think it does, then change," Bob said. "You will probably want to look at what is causing you to act this way." Then Hilda talked for two hours about her tragic childhood. Despite unbelievable disadvantages, she had become a successful speaker. Still, she felt inadequate, insecure, and fearful. She constantly worried that others would reject her or find out that she was just a fraud, so she put on a front of being confident and in control. After revealing her true feelings to Bob, she finally admitted that she also drank too much alcohol.

"Without a spiritual connection and with an alcohol problem, you are setting yourself up for appearing condescending and arrogant," Bob told her. Hilda agreed to set goals to find a spiritual connection and to overcome her drinking. One of the first things she did was to apologize to Abbie. Within a few weeks, everyone could see a wonderful change in Hilda.

In communicating her true feelings to Bob, Hilda took a big risk—but it paid off. She took another risk in accepting the hard truth that Bob and others had told her and in working to bring about changes in her thoughts, her words, and her actions with others. When Hilda started risking assertiveness and stopped being aggressive, she no longer had to worry so much about what others thought about her.

COME SAIL WITH US

Once when we were in Nassau on a speaking assignment, we had a free afternoon for sight-seeing. Walking on the beach, we saw, for the first time in our lives, two parasailers. High in the sky, they soared like exotic seagulls held up by multicolored parachutes. Tethered by a long rope to boats, they were being towed all around the bay. Bob took one look and knew he had to do it.

"Not me," Jane said, "but you go ahead."

Bob made his arrangements and rode out in the boat to a wooden pier that rose twenty feet out of the water. Attendants strapped him into a harness and parachute pack, and hooked the harness to the towing rope. They instructed him on how to take off and land.

"When we give the signal, just take one step off the pier," they said. Bob looked at the water so far below and gulped.

"I can't do that!" he thought, but he realized that if he didn't, the boat would pull him off. So he risked stepping into the empty air and was immediately sucked up into the sky. Below he could see all of Nassau, the beautiful blue bay, and even the fish in the clear waters. He felt as carefree as the fluffy white clouds all around him.

"It was a real high," Bob remembers. "When I came back I was so exhilarated that I told Jane she had to do it too. When she saw how excited I was, she became willing to take the risk. She loved it just as much as I did."

We both agreed that if we had not taken that first step off the pier, we could never have experienced that high. The same thing is true when you need to change your behavior in order to get off the worry-go-round. Something inside reacts with fear to giving up control of familiar thoughts, words, and actions, even though they hold you earthbound. By refusing to take that step off the secure pier, you cheat yourself of the wonderful feeling of freedom that is there for the asking.

It may seem scary to you to become completely honest about your feelings, tell them to another person, and then try out new, assertive behavior. If it does, we hope you will consider how much more beautiful the view becomes when you learn to risk.

CHAPTER 10

◆ ◆ ◆

The Fifth SKILL Tool:
Let Go of Problems

Mary Frances Burleson, a friend from Bob's Toastmasters days, deals with worry in a way that has served her well. Beginning in 1958 as a secretary at Ebby Halliday, Inc., one of Dallas's largest reality companies, she progressed to president in 1989.

"Worrying is as much a part of most people's nature as breathing. There is always something in the back of your mind whether you are aware of it or not. To combat it, I play the submarine game. I see my mind as a submarine with compartments. If water gets into one compartment, I seal it off so that I can still keep afloat. In other words, if I'm sitting at home in the midst of a crisis, I concentrate all my efforts on solving that crisis. I seal off the concerns about my work in another compartment, knowing that I can take action on them later. Then when I leave home to go to work, I open up the work compartment and shut off the compartment that contains my home worries, because I know that I have no way to take action on them at the office. While I am driving, I am zeroing in on what is going to happen on the job, who I'm going to see that day, and what problems need my

127

attention. In the evening, on the way home, I segment my thoughts once again," she told us.

Through her submarine game, Mary Frances is using the techniques of our Fifth SKILL Tool by distancing herself from problems when she cannot take action on them. Judging from her comments, this philosophy helps her progress in her career and keep her peace of mind at home and on the job. Here is the way we phrase it:

♦ *The Fifth SKILL Tool: Let Go of Problems.*

By letting go, we don't mean refusing to take action on a problem. Dr. Rege Stewart, a psychiatrist at Southwestern Medical School in Dallas, says, "By translating your concern into action or a resolution, you can stop the negative effects of worry. You must separate the concerns over which you have control from those which you cannot change. If you don't have any control, you must accept the situation."

This is why the Fourth SKILL Tool, which teaches you to be assertive, set goals, and risk new behavior, comes before the Fifth. When you know that you have done all that you can, and the problem is still with you, then you can use the Fifth Tool: simply let go of your concern. Easier said than done? Yes, but with Fifth Tool skills, you will find that you can do it. When you do let go, you will find a new calm way to live that actually enables you to solve problems you hadn't believed had any solutions.

THE TIMES YOU NEED TO LET GO

On a trip to tiny Fredericksburg, Texas, home of Chester W. Nimitz, commander of the U. S. Pacific Fleet during World War II, Pauline was impressed when she read the words of wisdom that that great naval hero treasured during the battles of the Southwest Pacific: "The sea, like life itself, is a stern taskmaster," his grandfather had told him when he was a little boy. "The best way to get along with either is to learn all you can, do your best, and *don't worry, especially over things over which you have no control.*" (Italics ours.) Few of us today have to deal with the battles Nimitz faced, but nearly everyone has to deal with problems over which they have no control.

Karen told her focus group that one of her biggest worries was what to do about the bickering that went on constantly between her husband and his sister.

"Invariably when the family got together, my husband and his sister ended up not speaking. I worried about what effect their fighting had on my children. I worried about why I couldn't solve their problems. It seemed that if I were just loving enough to both of them, then they wouldn't fight. I tried everything I could, but the only result was that I would get tied up in knots and they would still be angry. Finally I decided that their fights were their business, not mine. I sat down and had a little talk with each one of them separately. I told them that I loved them and wanted to be on good terms with them and that their relationship with each other was their responsibility, not mine. If they got mad at each other, I wasn't going to try to patch things up any more. I would let them settle it. They still fight, but not as much as they used to. And when they are angry, I keep my cool."

No one can change the behavior of other people, but women who are on the nurturing path to worry often think they can. They work very hard to control other people, worry a lot about them, and change nothing. By letting go of the urge to control others, you can find peace of mind for yourself and facilitate growth for others.

Kelly needed to let go for a different reason. In an auto accident Kelly received a head injury that left her unable to continue in her career as an attorney. She had to return to college and study a new vocation. Kelly worried about her loss of independence and her future. What if she couldn't make good enough grades to keep her scholarship? What if she couldn't support herself in the new career? What if she had to depend on her parents and sister to help her forever? A support group helped Kelly realize that depending on other people was not always bad. "People need people, and you are lucky to have someone who loves you," they told her. "If you let go of your worries, you will do better in school."

Sometimes, as in Kelly's case, life really is a stern taskmaster. If you get socked with chronic health problems, accidents, or burdens created by loved ones, you can worry about these injustices and create more problems for yourself by just dwelling on them, or you can learn to let go. Look at your worry and ask yourself:

- Is this situation one that will be affected if I take action?
- Is this situation one that can be solved only if other people take action?
- Is this situation one which no one can change?

Only if you answer yes to the first question and no to the other two do you have any control. If these were your answers, refer to the other four SKILL Tools and risk making changes. If you answered no to the first question and yes to the other two, we hope you'll master the Fifth SKILL Tool and learn how to let go.

WHY YOU NEED TO LET GO

Remember your old "friend," Mr. Negative, who keeps calling on you? If you continue to worry after you have done all you can, you are informing your unconscious, "I want to have more problems." Your unconscious listens and sends you depression, migraines, or other stress-related illnesses. It opens you to bitterness, anger, guilt, and fear. It causes you to fail at whatever you are doing.

When Bob was learning to play golf, he discovered a secret that most professional athletes use. Once you have prepared yourself to play by studying how to grip the club, position your feet, and tilt your shoulder; once you have practiced the technique, then you need to step up to the tee and *let go*. If instead you worry about whether you will hit the ball into the water hazard, your unconscious will make sure that you do so. By letting go of tension and worry, you can be relaxed and fluid. By letting instinct and technique operate unhindered by mental static, you can make the proper swing. After letting go, you will be much more likely to make a hole in one.

Letting go generates *positive expectancy*—the signal to your unconscious to create solutions and peaceful feelings. The mother who at midnight is worried because her teenage son has not come home has no control over what is happening to him. She can worry herself into a panic or she can visualize him driving into the garage, perfectly safe and happy. She can see him walking in the door. By refusing to answer when Mr. Negative calls, you create positive expectancy. You become a part of the solution rather than a part of the problem, and you are freed from the worry-go-round. Then, if something bad does happen, you have the energy you need to focus on taking swift, sure action.

Now that you know when and why to let go, we will teach you *how* to let go. These techniques will help you change yourself rather than fruitlessly try to change others.

LETTING GO BY ANALYZING YOUR EXPECTATIONS

With the Fourth SKILL Tool, we encouraged you to dream extravagantly and then set goals to achieve your dreams. The Fifth SKILL Tool helps you to determine when these expectations are unrealistic. Irene spent a lot of time on the worry-go-round because at forty, she and her husband had not been able to buy a six-bedroom mansion with a swimming pool. "Somehow, I always thought we would have the home of our dreams by the time we were this age. I feel like a failure. I worry about what's going to happen in the future," she told her focus group. Even though in our seminars we encourage people to dream big, Irene had unrealistic *positive expectations* that were causing her to worry and she had to let go of them.

If you have any *negative expectations*, you need to let go of these too. Kate told her focus group that she worried constantly about whether her performance at work was adequate. "I've never been criticized, but I worry anyway," she said. Kate's negative expectations were unrealistic. Ironically, they were draining her of the optimism and energy she needed to continue doing a good job.

When a desire or a fear is causing you anxiety, ask yourself these questions:

1. *Is my desire or fear realistic?* Since Irene and her husband had never made a six-figure income even though both worked, their dream of a mansion was unrealistic. Take a look at your strengths

and weaknesses. If you are really good at something, pat yourself on the back and enjoy your healthy self-esteem. Go ahead and dream, set goals, and visualize success. But if your dream is based on an activity in which you are weak, and the lack of results is worrying you, let go of that dream, modify it, or change your expectations and concentrate on the things that you can do. Irene and her husband had a good marriage which they could better enjoy if Irene gave up her disappointment over not being wealthy.

To determine whether your negative expectations are realistic, look at past events. Ask yourself if the catastrophe you are predicting has ever happened before. If it hasn't, you will know that it is unrealistic. Since Kate had never received a poor performance rating, her expectation that she would be criticized was unrealistic. If you are worried that your teenage daughter is going to get pregnant, do all you can to prevent that from happening. Express your concern and fears. Then ask yourself, "Has this ever happened before?" If it hasn't, cancel out this white-is-black thinking and replace it with positive visualizations and affirmations.

2. *Is my expectation for others logical?* Because Kate had low self-esteem, she expected others to criticize her. This was illogical, since no one had criticized her in the past. Because Irene had never been taught to solve her own problems, she hoped to be rescued by someone. She expected her husband somehow to be able to produce the home of her dreams. This was illogical, since neither he nor she produced the income needed for the mansion.

3. *Is my expectation about myself rational?* Kate looked at the Top Ten Basic Distortions (see chapter 9) and realized that she was practicing perfectionism and rejectionitis when she expected others to criticize her. Irene was refusing the positives by looking at the perfectly adequate home in which she was living and telling herself that it wasn't good enough. She also was thinking in should and ought legalisms by telling herself that because she was forty she should have the home of her dreams.

Recently Jane caught herself worrying about what other people would think if she appeared at the National Speakers Association convention in the same dress she had worn at the last convention.

"I asked myself those three questions. I realized how unrealistic and negative my expectation was that the 1250 people who attend those conventions would remember what I wore the year before. And even if they did, so what? Would people gather in corners and whisper about me? I was practicing perfectionism, rejectionitis, should and ought legalisms—practically all of the Top Ten Cognitive Distortions, because I was worrying about what other people would think," Jane said. "Once I analyzed my worry, I had to laugh at myself a little—which was a big help in letting go."

Jane was able to let go of her illogical expectation by analyzing it, noting her distorted thinking, and then restructuring her thinking.

4. *How important does my worry seem when I consider my whole lifetime?* If you worry that you have not fulfilled an expectation for yourself, or even *that* you have failed badly, sit down with a piece of paper and draw a time line for your entire life, the future included. Assume that you will live to a ripe old age. Mark off each of your eighty-odd years and then place a dot to represent the period when your failed expectation affected you. Very likely, you will see that it is a very small part of your life.

Let's say you have failed a course in college, lost your job or gotten divorced. Even if you worry about the event for two or three years, this amount of time is really very small when compared to the rest of your life. Others will forget your failure far more quickly than you. If you don't believe this is true, try to remember the details of all the mass murders you ever read about. Terrible, weren't they? Yet you have likely forgotten who committed them and exactly how. Your "terrible failure" is simply an unfulfilled expectation. When you let go of it, you will be able to see that you have many more years in which to do great things.

5. *What is my payoff for worrying about this situation?* Sometimes worry is a way of not taking real responsibility for ourselves. When Kate worried about her job performance, she became a workaholic to make sure that her work would be perfect. She spent day and night either catching up on her backlog or checking insignificant details. The payoff was that with all her time occupied, no one could expect her to have much of a social life. She didn't have to improve her appearance or practice being assertive in social situations because she was just too busy with her work. Irene's payoff also had to do with not facing up to low self-esteem: She was

putting all her self-worth into material things rather than developing her talents as a caring and responsible human being.

In trying to figure out the payoff to your worry, ask yourself how the Three Lacks might be involved. Like our friend, Gilda, you may at first tell yourself that there is no ulterior motive to your worrying. Gilda wanted desperately to succeed as an entrepreneur. When her business went into the red for several months, she started worrying so much that she felt that she was on the verge of a breakdown. Gilda recognized that she had a legitimate concern that she might lose her business, but why was she overreacting to the point of losing her health? By using the "So What!" Technique outlined in chapter 6, she found that she perceived a business failure as a personal inadequacy. "*I'm* a failure, I should be doing better than I am," she was telling herself. As a little girl Gilda had been taught to be a pleaser and look pretty; if she did that, others would solve her problems for her. The payoff for her worry now was to see *herself* as the failure, not the business. If she were the culprit, she could give up and someone would rescue her. She wouldn't have to risk hanging on in her business, working long hours, and finding more profitable ways to operate.

When Gilda looked at the situation assertively, she realized that no one was going to rescue her. Telling herself that she was a failure was only harming her self-esteem and impairing her ability to function. She decided to stop answering Mr. Negative. Then she saw what had been obvious all along. Her business was suffering because the economy of the whole area was down. In fact, when she averaged out her income for the year she saw that she was ahead of many.

"When I recognized what I was doing to my self-esteem, I decided it was better to let go of my business expectations rather than to put myself down. I was a worthy person no matter what happened. I would either go bankrupt or the economy would get better. Either way, I knew that I could survive and that I was okay."

We have made the point throughout this book that it is good to dream great dreams and to visualize success. We still believe that positive expectancy will generate many good things for you. If, however, your expectations—be they positive or negative— are causing you to worry or are undermining your self-esteem, then the wise thing to do is to let go of them.

LIVING IN THE PRESENT MOMENT

A friend whom we'll call Kathy, who lives on the West Coast, telephoned one day to tell us her worries. Her husband had lost his job. On top of that, her sales commissions were down. She was afraid they would have to move. Life was bleak, and she could see nothing in her future but catastrophe.

"Kathy, just do one thing for me today," Bob told her. "Go out to that beautiful beach, take a walk and thank God that you can be in such a wonderful place. Then think about the fact that you are healthy, bright, and attractive. Be grateful that you have what it takes to move forward in the future."

Later, Kathy telephoned us to thank us. Her anxiety had lessened considerably, simply because Bob had reminded her how liberating it can be to *live in the present moment*. Her mind became so filled with enjoyment of the Pacific Coast loveliness and assessment of all the positive things that were going on in her life that there was no room in it for predictions of doom.

When you are worried about some terrible thing that has happened to you and are ruminating about how it is going to affect you in the future, use the Present Moment Technique. Remind yourself that the past is over and done with and that you can't predict or control the future. You can only affect yourself and the things around you in the very moment in which you now find yourself.

Jane learned this lesson when she moved to Dallas in the eighties. "I hated Texas. All my life I had lived in the little village of Clemmons, North Carolina. I missed my friends and family. I told myself I was never going to be happy in Dallas." Jane was so miserable that she telephoned people in North Carolina every day. The only thing she did with her time was to count the days until she could visit her "home." When she telephoned one lifelong friend and poured out her troubles for the umpteenth time, the friend simply said, "Don't you think you should let your mind join your body in Texas?"

At first Jane was not grateful for this confrontation, but she did have to recognize that she was living in the past and worrying about the future. To make her new neighborhood seem more like home, she decided to accept the fact that she no longer lived in

North Carolina. She took action by finding a good drugstore and supermarket. She looked for friends. Soon Jane found the pearl in her worry: She understood for the first time that she was accountable for her own happiness. This understanding led her to a new career that she loved, marriage to Bob, and Life Plus.

Living in the present moment functions as a distraction from worry. The mind cannot think of more than one thing at a time. If you let imaginary catastrophic scenarios fade from your mental screen and focus on the positive things that are happening to you at this very moment, you almost *can't* worry. Counting your blessings to lift your mood is folk wisdom that still works.

To become more aware of the good things in your life, write down every positive thing you can think of about yourself. List your good qualities and don't be modest. Are you a loving person? Do you have special talents? Think of creature comforts. Do you have enough to eat and a roof over your head? Consider the people in your life who mean something to you. Do you have loved ones? Friends? Focus on what you have rather than what you lack. Whenever you start to worry about something over which you have no control, take out your list and read it.

TAKING TIME TO WORRY

If you have tried your best to distract yourself from your worry and still find yourself taking fearful thoughts into your consciousness and grinding away at them, then put limits on the amount of time you will worry. Set aside thirty minutes each day to worry as hard as you can. Find a private place, close the door, and devote yourself to imagining the most terrible catastrophes you can create. Use the brainstorming strategies from chapter 7 to get all your worries out in the open. Admit to them all—even the *most* irrational ones! Then thank each one of them for the special gift that it will bring you and affirm your ability to find the gift.

Kathy, our West Coast friend with the financial problems, thanked her worry. First she described the worry by writing it down in her notebook: "I am worried about lack of money and the possibility of having to move." Next she thanked her worry this way: "I know you're trying to help me discover work opportunities

I have never considered before and to open me to a more relaxed way to live." Next she affirmed herself by writing: "I like relaxing by walking on the beach and I am getting some good ideas about how to handle the problems." Kathy found it a relief to go through this exercise so that she could say good-bye to her worry.

After thanking your worry and affirming yourself as Kathy did, you can let go of the worry for the rest of the day. Immediately move on to other thoughts. Begin an activity that requires your concentration. You might sign up for a course or lecture series or take up folk dancing, crafts, or some other new interest. Find something that you can enjoy and do it as hard as you can. With your mind filled with exciting new activities, it won't have room for worry.

Another way to keep yourself in the present moment is to ask someone who thinks positively to help you. Be sure to avoid worry partners. Tell your chosen friend that you want help in identifying all the good things in your life.

LETTING GO BY VISUALIZING

Ever since Kristin's home was flooded during a terrible storm, she panics whenever she hears rain. She can't stop worrying that the water will rise so high that she will be drowned. Once, when Kristin was worrying over the rain, her husband told her, "Kristin, it's okay. If the water comes into the house, we'll go to higher ground. We'll go into the attic." This was such a comforting thought that Kristin often repeats it to herself whenever she hears the first raindrop. She visualizes herself high up in the attic, safe from the swirling waters, which she always visualizes as receding rather than rising.

We think Kristin's husband's advice is good for everyone. Whenever you are worried, go to higher ground. Make use of your unconscious to visualize yourself safe, happy, healthy, and free of problems.

We have improvised on the the pink bubble visualization which Shakti Gawain describes in *Creative Visualization* to apply it to letting go of worry. Pink is the color associated with the heart and, consequently, with emotions. If you are worried about what loved ones are doing and you need to let go of this because it is beyond your control, simply visualize them looking happy and loving. Surround them with a beautiful pink bubble. Then see the bubble floating off into space while you affirm that all is well. When you release your worry to the positive forces in the universe, you will feel more peace of mind. Your positive outlook and peace of mind will undoubtedly have a positive effect on your loved ones.

You can also use humorous visualizations to help you let go. In their helpful book, *Not to Worry*, Mary McClure Goulding and Robert L. Goulding advise converting the endings of your worry scenarios to make them fantastic, fun, or ludicrously tragic. For instance, if you worry that you won't be able to afford college for your daughter, you could use fantasy to see her receiving money from leprechauns or Martians from outer space. Or you could make your visualization fun by imagining your daughter seeking her fortune in a faraway jungle rather than at college, discovering a new kind of sugar that has no calories which brings her boundless wealth. Or you could make your visualization ludicrously tragic by imagining your daughter so poor that she is dressed in rags, holding a starving baby, and begging crusts of bread. When you realize how ridiculous these scenarios are, you will have to laugh; when you laugh, you can't worry.

Jocelyn told us about a ludicrously tragic visualization that she created when the man she thought was going to be hers for life suddenly moved out of their apartment. At first Jocelyn cried and raged to her friends about what a Number One, Class A rat this man was. She told them that she never wanted to see him again. Then he called.

"You're still special to me. Can't we be friends? I'd like to come over tonight," he said. Jocelyn wavered. Her heart wanted to say yes, but her mind knew that he would only be using her and that she would be doubly hurt in the end. She told him no, but worried that she would not have enough strength of character to keep from being manipulated if he called again. So she created an image of herself that kept her from worrying and prevented her from giving in. She saw herself as a person with no skin at all. She was virtually a big piece of raw meat. If anyone tried to touch her, it would feel like vinegar being poured into a wound. This fantasy worked. She was able to let go of the worry and the desire to see her former lover long enough to work through her grief and anger. She was able to build her self-worth. Eventually Jocelyn was able to forgive her former boyfriend and become a whole person again.

LETTING GO BY FORGIVING

An old Chinese proverb says, "If you want revenge, dig two graves." One of the graves is for the person who hurt you; the other is for you. When you worry over a past grievance, or when you get stuck in fantasizing about all the terrible things you hope will happen to that person who did you wrong, you trigger feelings of shame and guilt. In this way, the desire for revenge ultimately corrodes your self-esteem. If you have suffered a significant loss, you may not be able to forgive immediately. You may have to set a goal to forgive and then work through your grief and rage. While Jocelyn was visualizing herself as raw meat, she tried to get revenge on her former boyfriend, a fireman, by fantasizing that he was being roasted like a marshmallow every time she heard a siren. Jocelyn discovered that while this visualization seemed justified by her rage, it brought her no good feelings about herself. To reclaim her wholeness and peace of mind, she had to let go of vindictive thoughts; she had to forgive.

To us, true forgiveness is feeling as if the wrong truly never happened. It is replacing anger with love. At a recent seminar, we heard about a way to visualize forgiveness that we believe is helpful after you have worked through some of the immediate anger. Close your eyes and create your Higher Self: being and acting as the most perfectly loving person you can imagine. Now create the one you want to forgive in his or her Higher Self. Then let these two Higher Selves sit down and talk about the painful situation. What would they say to each other about what happened? Every time you fall back into thinking negatively about that person, immediately go back to this visualization, picturing and hearing your Higher Self's words. Eventually you will be able to forgive. Like Jocelyn, you will feel like a whole person again.

We recognize that there are some truly hateful people in this world at whose hands women often suffer real wrongs. Sometimes you have to cut your losses and sever your connection with such people. Could you ever forgive someone who has committed a violent crime against you or a loved one? To overcome the anxiety of rehashing the past, you should work very hard to forgive. If you really cannot, then use the Present Moment technique to protect your own mental and physical health.

EVERYBODY HAS SCARS

Often when Jane speaks before the public, she tells her story of being burned as a child. "I don't know whether I could see your scars as you could see mine if we were together. Scars sometimes are invisible when they come from worry, illness, or chaotic relationships, yet we all have them. Everyone we come in contact with has scars," she says.

Invariably people come to her afterward to tell her about their scars. Some have suffered through unbelievable childhoods.

"I sometimes think that the story of my childhood is nothing compared to theirs," Jane says. "But I always tell them, 'No matter what your scars are, you are beautiful on the inside. When you believe that and act on it, your scars will not only bear witness to your pain, but also to your healing.' "

We don't have any control over the scars in our lives. Try as hard as we might, we can't erase them. We can only let go of them and accept the fact that we are beautiful inside. We hope that our Fifth SKILL Tool will allow you to do that.

PART III

◆ ◆ ◆

Using the SKILL
Tools to Stop
Specific Worries

CHAPTER 11

♦ ♦ ♦

Taking the Worry Out of Finances and Career Issues

Now that you have learned how to use the SKILL Tools, we want to show how you can apply them to the worries associated with specific problems. Since our focus groups tell us that finances and career issues cause their biggest worries, we will begin with those.

Not having enough money to pay the bills was the number one concern of the women who participated in these groups. Women also told us that they climbed on the worry-go-round because they:

- Lacked money for retirement or for unforeseen emergencies or illnesses
- Were unable to break through the glass ceiling and progress in a career
- Overspent their monies
- Had no man to help provide income
- Struggled with a business failure or loss of a job

"After my divorce," Louise told her focus group, "my life turned upside down in more ways than one, but especially in money matters. I couldn't find a good job, so I worried constantly about how I was going to pay the bills. Even worse, I discovered that I didn't *want* to be the one who balanced the checkbook or figured the income tax or saw that the house and car were adequately insured or called the repair service when the air conditioner broke. I just wanted to run to the beach every weekend and play. I put off dealing with those problems as long as I could, and the longer I procrastinated, the more I worried. I lay awake every night, sleepless with fear."

Like many women, Louise was not prepared to make financial decisions. As a child, her father had made them for her and her mother. After she was married, she was all too willing to let her husband take over. When she found herself facing financial responsibilities alone, she felt inadequate.

Louise was equally unprepared for a career. The low-level corporate job that she finally found did not pay enough to enable her to live at the same standard as that when she had been married. Louise felt angry that she earned less money than men who had the same qualifications as she did. She saw no opportunities for promotion. When she tried to be assertive, male coworkers told her she was being "bitchy." No wonder Louise just wanted to forget about financial problems and run to the beach!

The facts are, however, that financial problems don't wash out to sea while you tan yourself on the sand. If you don't deal with bills and career challenges, you will find yourself, like Louise, immobilized by worry.

WHY WOMEN WORRY ABOUT FINANCES

While women face many different kinds of financial problems, we believe that financial worries stem from the Three Lacks described in chapter 6, as well as some special societal influences:

• Low self-esteem keeps women from risking assertive actions, such as communicating openly with business associates, going into business for themselves, or learning how to manage their own money. Passivity leads to frequent failures and a loss of self-confidence.

- Society penalizes women in the workplace by paying them less, as well as requiring them to take most of the responsibility for nurturing children, and providing less opportunity for promotion.
- Women are not raised to make decisions and solve problems about finances.

While we can make it a long-range goal to change society, our SKILL Tools can help you today to overcome the Three Lacks and become more assertive about pursuing financial security. When enough women give up being passive and afraid to share their creative ideas with the world, society will change.

LOOKING AT THE PLUSSES

Despite the fact that many little girls are not raised to see themselves as financial successes, all you have to do is to look around you to see that many women have already made it in the financial world.

Home economist Karen Johnson joined the Pillsbury Company in 1962. Her goal was to become director of the refrigerated test kitchens at that company, according to a profile in the May 1989 issue of *Working Woman* magazine. She not only reached that goal, she went on to become a corporate vice-president of the Borden Company and a member of the CEO's top management group. Karen reached this pinnacle of success by first preparing herself with degrees in dietetics, food, nutrition, and a diploma from Le Cordon Bleu in Paris. Then she watched how the top (all male) Pillsbury executives performed. She risked using the same management skills.

"I learned how to position what I want to say," she told *Working Woman*. She learned to give constructive criticism rather than trying to please everyone and refused to worry about whether she was well liked. She even took on the difficult task of firing her best friend because of inferior performance. "I lost her as a friend," Johnson admits, but points out that as women move up the career ladder, "we may have to disappoint, displease—even anger—others."

Our friend Tanya did not have the extensive education to prepare for a career that Karen Johnson did, but she found something equally effective—a mentor. When Tanya had five small children, her husband deserted her. Faced with being the chief breadwinner and unable to pay for child care for five, she began selling anything she could find—from Tupperware and Amway products to real estate—that would allow her to work out of her home. One day, after listening to a successful realtor speak on effective sales techniques, she told him, "I'd sure like to do what you do." When she told him about herself, he invited her to join his sales staff. She did, and he taught her many invaluable skills. Eventually she set out on her own and became a multimillionaire. Along the way, she remarried and had three more children while continuing in her various sales enterprises.

Could either of these women have achieved their remarkable successes in the business world if they had been frozen with worry, feeling unable to make decisions or solve problems, feeling that they were worthless or frauds? We think not. They are living proof that if you want to progress in a career or simply to support yourself in a comfortable manner, many opportunities are open to you, despite societal barriers. The choice about whether to remain stuck in worry or to take creative action is yours.

APPLYING THE FIRST SKILL TOOL TO FINANCIAL WORRIES

Your first step in applying the SKILL Tools to financial worries is to sit down with your journal and write out your financial problem. Perhaps it is not having enough money to pay the bills or to save for your children's future college expenses or to build your retirement fund. Perhaps you have suffered a business failure or you don't have a job. Whatever it is, write it down.

Now apply the First SKILL Tool: Seek the real reason for your worry, so that you can make an accurate diagnosis of your problem. Write down all the reasons why you think you have this problem. You might write: "My expenses are greater than my income," or "We had unexpected medical bills," or "A single parent just can't make it on one paycheck."

Now assess whether your worry is realistic by comparing the amount of money you receive with the amount you spend. Add all your fixed expenses, plus the estimated amount you consider necessary for clothing, food, recreation, household improvements, and any other category you feel is necessary. If your expenses exceed your income, you may believe that you have a simple problem: you just don't have enough money. By using the First SKILL Tool, however, you can also check to see whether you have a hidden agenda that prevents your figures from telling the whole truth. You may spend too much on nonfixed expenses because of a feeling of inadequacy or insecurity. For instance, ask yourself, "Do I really need another new pair of shoes to attract someone, or do I need to realize that I have plenty of attractive qualities simply because I am who I am?" or "Do I really need a new car now or am I using a car to impress others with my success rather than learning to accept myself as I am?"

Lisa told us that she thought she ought to be able to deal with her financial worries. "When I was growing up my parents helped me define problems and seek alternatives. I found that I could use their very logical process with worries that belonged to other people. When my own emotions were involved, however, I never found a good way to do this. Now I'm learning how to define what I *really* want, and that includes making rational decisions about spending."

To see whether any of the Three Lacks are affecting your spending habits, make four columns with headings for the Psychosocial, Instinctive, Societal, and Physiological Paths To Worry. Ask yourself if any of these apply to you. Under the Psychosocial heading, write down whether your self-perception influences the amount of money you spend on nonfixed expenses. Do you spend too much on clothing, cars, or cosmetics because you don't feel good about yourself and buying treats is a way to feel better? Do you find yourself believing that a man should handle your money problems?

Laura's husband was clearly irresponsible about money, but Laura was afraid to sit down and discuss a budget with him, because she knew he would fly into a rage. Besides, she had no experience in handling finances. While she was growing up, her father had always been the one who managed the money. When she got married, it seemed natural for her husband to be responsible for everything except a small household fund which he doled out to her once a week for the groceries. Besides, Laura told herself, it was not the woman's place to manage family finances. The only problem with this kind of passivity was that Laura had to live with fear of the bill collectors and with resentment toward her husband. She needed to learn to solve financial problems and also to increase her self-esteem so she could speak up assertively with her husband.

Under the Instinctive heading, ask yourself whether your desire to take care of others is running rampant. Are you spending too much on relatives and friends as a way of demonstrating that you care? Lee just couldn't stop buying clothes for her teenagers. They had closets full of the latest designer labels, while Lee lay awake at night worrying about how to pay the bills. She lacked the self-esteem to put her teenagers on a clothing budget and to hold them to it, especially if they became angry at her. She was afraid that people would think she was a "bad mother" if she required them to earn money for their clothes by doing household chores.

Under the Societal heading, ask yourself whether paying for day care leaves you with little take-home pay. Do household responsibilities take time away from your job so that you can't make as much money as you otherwise could? You may feel helpless to do anything about these societal problems, but write them down anyway and brainstorm some solutions. Ginger told her focus group that she solved these problems by becoming assertive enough to explore career options. When she found a better job that paid a higher salary, she could afford day care and help at home too.

Under the Physiological heading, ask yourself whether hormonal fluctuations make you feel so edgy and nervous that not having as much money as you would like seems to be an insurmountable problem. When you have PMS, do you use poor judgment about expenditures? If so, be assertive in seeking treatment. Schedule important financial decisions at a time when you feel well physically.

If you are riding the worry-go-round over a business failure, the real reason for your worry might be a fear of success. You really want to handle money wisely, but your unconscious tells you that you are not a competent person who deserves success, so you sabotage yourself and then stew about it. Or, you might be worried because you value yourself only in terms of your financial success. These are self-esteem issues.

Once you have explored the real reasons for your worry, write them down. Look for a worry theme. Is your worry tied to some traumatic childhood event like Bob's feeling that he was inferior because his slightly withered leg made him different from the other boys, or Jane's feeling that she was "the scarred one?" Use the "So what!" Technique to dig deeper.

For instance, Lee, the mother who spent too much on her children's clothing, might write:

> "If I don't spend a lot on my children's clothes, they won't be as well dressed as the other children at school."
> "So what?"
> "So I would feel like a bad mother."
> "So what?"
> "So I realize I'm spending money on them because of my own poor self-esteem and *my* need to look good, not theirs."

If after using the First SKILL Tool, you still believe that the problem is simply not having enough money, then you may not, in fact, have a hidden agenda. Write your diagnosis: "My problem is that I don't have enough money."

ALTERING, AVOIDING, AND ACCEPTING WITH THE SECOND SKILL TOOL

Now you are ready to use the Second SKILL Tool: Know your alternatives. Label three pages in your journal with "Alter," "Avoid," and "Accept." Then brainstorm a prescription for action that will heal your diagnosed worry. Write down everything, no matter how ridiculous it may seem. If you can't think of any productive alternatives, seek out a positive, action-oriented person—not a worry partner—to help you.

Alternatives for altering might include going to work if you have been a housewife, getting a second job, learning new skills for a better job, or setting more realistic budget goals. Our friend Irene chose the alternative of cutting expenses. She started cleaning her apartment herself instead of paying someone else to do it. To increase her income, she started working for a wedding consultant on weekends.

Altering might mean finding a financial consultant. If you can't afford to pay for financial advice, ask your banker, a chamber of commerce financial counseling service, or a reputable agency (check the Better Business Bureau in case of any doubt) to help you consolidate your bills and set up a budget. You might also take a course in household finances or assertiveness training.

In the "Avoid" column you could write down: "I will learn more cost-conscious ways to shop. I'll start clipping coupons and waiting for sales to make purchases. I will attend a lecture on how to coordinate clothing so that I won't have to buy five pairs of different colored shoes every season."

Consider whether you are using credit cards as emotional bandages. Whenever you are hurting, lonesome, or sad, do you buy something to turn off your pain? We know a woman who makes a six-figure income who is in debt simply because she believes that she must never be seen in "something old." Every time she buys a new dress, she feels a real high! This "spendoholic" needs to throw away her credit cards, pay off her debt, and use another altering tool—distraction. She can replace her addiction to buying clothes with a satisfying new hobby or doing things for others that will make her feel good about herself. She must also learn to say no to Mr. Negative when he tells her she is unworthy unless she is dressed in the latest fashion.

Under the "Accept" column, you can select the attitudinal healing tool and write "It is true that I don't know where the money will come from to pay my bills, but I recognize that if I give up unrealistic expectations rather than nag at myself and imagine catastrophes, I will worry less. I'll make a goal to let go."

After you have exhausted all the alternatives you can think of, promise yourself that you will set a goal to accomplish at least three of your solutions.

IMAGING FINANCIAL GOALS WITH THE THIRD SKILL TOOL

With the Third SKILL Tool, you will make use of the imaginative power of your unconscious mind. Make a goal sheet that states your goal in a positive manner in the present tense. For instance, you might write "I know how to manage money," or "I am receiving plenty of money to meet all my needs," or "I am enjoying living within my budget."

Next, write how you will visualize and affirm your goals. You might see yourself with a large balance in your checkbook after you have paid the bills, or you might visualize your handbag overflowing with $100 bills. You might see yourself enrolling in a money management seminar or being able to put $20 in your college tuition fund each week. To stop being a spendoholic, visualize a big red X over the door to your favorite store. Affirm that you have plenty of money to meet all your needs.

Write how you will act *as if*: "I will talk about positive things rather than my money worries." "I will wear my nicest clothes and act as if I have no money worries." "I will involve myself in hobbies rather than spending."

Leave space on your goal sheet to check off the times you go to alpha and reprogram your unconscious with visualizations every day. Write down "atta girl" whenever you think you've done a good job—and that means every day if possible.

When Bob first started wanting to change from a negative to a positive person so that he could overcome his agoraphobia, she read Napoleon Hill's *Think and Grow Rich*. He took to heart Hill's axiom: "Whatever the mind can conceive and believe, the mind can achieve." He found that it helped him become a more confident, positive person who could recover from agoraphobia. Later he found that he could use his conscious mind to conceive of financial success as a professional speaker, even though he had a fear of facing an audience. First Bob reprogrammed his unconscious to help him believe that he could be free of fear when he made a speech and that he would actually be paid for speaking. He set a goal to learn speech skills at Toastmasters and visualized himself being well received there. He worked hard to do so. Step by step he set goals to progress in his career, always visualizing success and taking the necessary action. Because he convinced his unconscious that he could excel in a new career, he was able to achieve his goal.

We find that many women who want to be financially secure sabotage their efforts with poor self-esteem. They just don't believe that they "deserve" to be rich. That was certainly the case with a very capable speaker whom we will call Lois, who received a contract from a Fortune 500 company for $30,000 to conduct a month-long series of training seminars. At first Lois was thrilled. She had never made so much money in thirty days in her life. She led the seminars, went home, and then did not earn another fee for a speech for six months.

"I just couldn't believe I was worth $30,000 for a single month's work. I felt like a fraud. I even had nightmares about it. I would dream that an official from the company that hired me told me I had done a terrible job and that he was taking the money back. I was so wrapped up in worry about my 'failure' that I couldn't bear to ask other companies to use me as a trainer," she told us.

Lois has cheated herself out of the success she deserves simply because she doesn't believe in herself. She needs to set a goal to increase her self-esteem and affirm that this company paid her $30,000 because she could do what they asked of her and that to them her special talents were worth the price. She needs to visualize herself standing in front of her audience, receiving a standing ovation.

We can't emphasize enough how important it is to have positive expectations about your goals. When you create a goal sheet for financial success, dream in a big way! When your dreams come true, congratulate yourself and move on to even greater accomplishments.

HOW MUCH ARE YOU WILLING TO RISK?

The Fourth SKILL Tool enables you to risk taking action on your goals. Review the alternatives you discovered when you applied the Triple A Formula to your financial problems. What were the altering, avoiding, and accepting goals that you listed? What were the action steps that you created when you imaged those goals? The Fourth Tool will help you take action on those goals.

Laura, the woman who had the financially irresponsible husband, faced up to her lack of self-esteem by setting a goal to stop being part of the "I'll Take Care of You" syndrome. She would learn how to manage money herself and then risk confronting her husband about his overspending. She took action by attending classes in assertiveness training and household finances at a community college. In the assertiveness class she saw that she had been thinking in terms of "mistaken identity" and "my fault." She had been telling herself that she really was incapable of managing finances because the men in her life had told her so. In addition, she had been assuming that it was her fault that her husband flew into rages over the money she spent on groceries.

"When I grew confident enough to stop removing the price labels from the packages of meat before I left the supermarket so that my husband wouldn't see them, I realized I was making progress. Eventually I risked telling him, 'I'm not willing for you to control our finances. I want to share the decisions.' " she said. Laura's assertiveness did not lead to an instant solution to this couple's differing philosophies about money, but it did convince her husband that they needed financial counseling. Laura's worries are fewer since she risked action to solve her financial problem.

Whether your goal is to earn plenty of money or to enjoy living within your budget, you can do the same thing that Laura did. Use the Fourth SKILL Tool and risk changing your thoughts, words, and actions. Once you have set your goals, make a daily checklist to be sure that you are acting on those goals, and congratulate yourself as you accomplish a little more each day. Laura's list might have looked like this:

1. I will stay within our budget for groceries by making meal plans and not buying extras we don't need.
2. I will go to an alpha state and see myself with a balanced checkbook and affirm that I am perfectly capable of handling my financial responsibilities myself.
3. Whenever my husband tells me I am too stupid to handle finances, I will remind him, "I will not accept being put down by you."

4. Whenever my husband and I discuss finances, I will communicate my feelings honestly. If he becomes angry, I will recognize that his feelings are his own responsibility, not mine.

LETTING GO OF FINANCIAL WORRIES

After Inga visited her sister in another state, she came home feeling more worried than ever about her financial problems. "My sister lives in a mansion, she has household help, and she can spend whatever she wants on the house and her children. That's what I always thought I would have too. I kept tearing myself up about not having it," she told her focus group. Inga and her husband both had good jobs, but they did not earn enough to live as her sister did. Inga had to give up her expectations of being wealthy before she could stop worrying about not having enough to live on.

"I was looking at what I didn't have rather than what I had," she now is able to say.

Are your financial worries beyond your control? If your own paycheck is too low, you have the power to do something about it. You can seek another job or work overtime. If your partner's income is too low, however, and he is unwilling to make changes, that problem is beyond your control. Like Inga, you may need to let go of that worry, count your blessings, and start living in the present moment. Develop interests that don't require credit cards.

If you can't seem to let go of money problems, try reversing your worry scenarios with fantasies. See all your bills in one stack, surrounded by a beautiful pink bubble. Then let the bubble float away while you affirm that your worries will be solved by the positive forces in the universe. Or use a ludicrous tragic opera approach: See yourself singing a mournful aria like "Vesti La Giubbale" while those to whom you owe money sharpen their daggers. When you can let go in this manner, you will sleep and think better—and you may feel free enough to see new solutions to some of the financial problems that you thought had no solutions.

WHY WOMEN WORRY ABOUT CAREERS

Women in our focus groups told us that their career worries centered around:

- Not being able to progress in the corporate structure
- Being branded "unfeminine" if they become assertive in the business world
- Being passed over for promotion if they aren't assertive enough
- Not having the same preparation to solve business problems that men have

"Being single with children, I can't hop on a plane and travel for the company without making extensive preparations," Lennie told her focus group. "Whenever they get sick, I am penalized for taking time off. Since the company makes no provision for parental responsibilities, I know that I will never get the promotions that I'm qualified for. I'm angry about that and I'm also worried, because I need the money for the support of my children."

For Cynthia the problem was not knowing how to compete with men. "After playing competitive sports as a boy, a man has learned how to confront a coworker with his mistakes, then go off to play golf with him and remain on the best of terms. I can't do that. I would worry that people wouldn't like me if I criticized them."

The fear of being thought unfeminine affects many business women. "I went in person to a firm that I had repeatedly billed for my fee," a professional woman told us. "When I told the president that I wanted my money, he said, 'Why are you being so hostile?' "

A corporate executive admitted that she worried over whether she should wear a red dress to the office. "Would that make me look too aggressive?" she asked. The worry for a lot of other women was the reverse. They were afraid of being branded "too feminine," by seeming unable to control their emotions.

Using the First SKILL Tool, consider whether the real reason for your career worries lies within yourself or society. While "old boy" networks may stand in the way of advancement, your perception of yourself as not being able to compete because you are a woman may indicate that you need to improve in assertiveness and problem-solving skills. If this is so, write it down.

ALTERNATIVES TO CAREER WORRIES

Using the Second SKILL Tool, ask yourself what you can alter, avoid, or accept about yourself and/or society that will help you get off the worry-go-round about your career.

Dallasite Ellen Terry altered her career worries by becoming assertive. She had to be: Fourteen years ago Ellen was married and enjoyed a luxurious lifestyle. She lived in a large Highland Park home and drove a Mercedes. Then one day while she was hosting a Junior League meeting, a burly man knocked on her door, asked which Mercedes was hers and repossessed it. Suddenly, without warning, the fairy tale life she had been living evaporated. She had to deal with the IRS, sell her furniture, jewelry, and clothes and move into a one-bedroom efficiency apartment. She had to begin doing her washing at a laundromat.

Virtually penniless, Ellen looked at her alternatives and decided that she could stick her head in the sand like an ostrich and remain that way or develop a career for herself.

She went to work for a short time in a travel agency and took courses on the weekends to become a realtor. When she looks back, she realizes it wasn't easy. The hardest part of all was sending her children to live with their grandparents. But her sacrifices paid off, because eventually Ellen had her own real estate firm, specializing in premier high-end homes in the area where she had once lived. Ellen believes that adversities are merely challenges that can be turned into opportunities for growth.

"If you don't like your circumstances, change yourself and you will get different circumstances," Ellen says. "In order for a butterfly to be able to fly, it has to stop being a caterpillar."

To avoid worries on the job, a good alternative might be to learn some skills. Lucille, a corporate executive, studied time management techniques at a seminar. Now she puts all her appointments, including business, personal, and free time activities, on one Daytimer. This book goes in her purse so that it is always available to write down a time commitment the moment she makes it.

"I used to have three or four calendars—one at the office, one at home and one in my handbag," Lucille said. "I didn't trust myself to keep up with all those different calendars, so I worried about trivial things such as missing a beauty appointment or a lunch with friends. This may not sound like a big deal, but I don't need to add trivia to the big worries I have on the job. Furthermore, I now write down my business expenses for each day in my Daytimer. At the end of the week, I total the number of miles I have driven on business and staple all the deductible receipts to my Daytimer. At the end of the year, I can assemble all the information my accountant requires for my income tax in a couple of nights," she said.

"Avoid the trap of worrying about titles, career moves, and networking," advised Barbara Kotlikoff, president of Parfums Nina Ricci U.S.A., Inc., in the June 1989 issue of *Cosmopolitan*. "The fastest road to success lies in completing day-to-day assignments crisply and intelligently. Focus your energy and talent on the project at hand, and the rewards will follow. If they don't, take your newfound ability to where it will be appreciated."

Sometimes the accepting alternatives are the most important. If you have children (or are planning to have them) and you are trying to become a partner in a firm of lawyers or CPAs, you may need to look at the situation realistically. We believe that there is no way for a woman to work the seventy- to eighty-hour weeks these firms require unless she has someone to care for the children or unless her husband is willing to assume many of the child-rearing responsibilities. The only solution that society offers at present seems to be following or not following the Mommy Track. You must decide early whether to have a time-consuming career with the chance of rapid advancement or children and a midlevel job with more flexible work hours. We do not agree that this is fair, but until the social structure changes, some alternatives are reducing your expectations, seeking a different career, or finding an enlightened corporation. If you feel that you must take action to change society, get involved in political or social movements that raise the consciousness of those in power.

IMAGING YOUR CAREER GOALS

When you have selected the alternatives that seem most appropriate for you, write them down and create visualizations and affirmations that will enlist your unconscious in carrying out your plan of action. See yourself receiving that promotion you want while your coworkers congratulate you.

If you have determined that the real reason for your career worry is a lack of confidence that makes you procrastinate, affirm "I enjoy making a sales call on _____ _____ (the difficult client)" or "It is perfectly acceptable for me to write a report that is less than perfect." If being emotional is your problem, visualize yourself looking confident and poised as you deal with difficult situations and people on the job. Affirm, "I am perfectly capable of carrying out my duties in a creative and excellent manner," and "I am calm and confident at all times."

Plan to go to an alpha state at least twice a day and repeat your visualizations and affirmations. Use them on the job whenever you run into an emotional emergency. Find a private spot, even if it has to be the restroom. Close your eyes, relax, and plug in to the wonderful help your unconscious has for you.

THE CAREER PAYOFF OF RISKING

By using the Fourth SKILL Tool and letting yourself risk action in your career, you will improve your chances for success. An article in the May 1989 issue of *Working Woman* magazine, for instance, reported that opportunities were plentiful in high technology companies for women who have the necessary skills *and tolerance for risk*. Kathryn Braun, a senior vice-president and general manager at Western Digital Corporation, was quoted as saying, "There's not much of an old boy network in this industry, because so many of the old boys are dead. It doesn't take long to be an instant success or, for that matter, an instant failure."

Risking action might also mean making the decision to avoid old boy networks entirely and become an entrepreneur. This is what many women, including Jane, have done, and the opportunities are wide open. During the eighties, women-owned businesses grew from 700,000 to 3 million in number. Government studies show that by the year 2000, the United States will have some 30 million enterprises, fully half of them owned by women. When you're the boss, you have the opportunity to break through the glass ceiling.

"In 1982, with a master's degree, I made only $25,000 a year even though I held a full-time teaching job in the public school, taught aerobic dancing at night, and tutored on the side," Jane says. "In the school system where I taught, only two women out of the 2,500 faculty members were principals. No women at all were on the administrative staff. It was clear that I was in a male-dominated institution in which women could serve only at the lower levels. Within three years after I went into business for myself, I could make three times as much," Jane says.

Jane cautions that in taking a risk, you sometimes have to take a step backward before you move ahead. During her first few months in business, Jane sold tapes for a professional speaker. Her income dropped from $2000 a month to $200 a month. Then she decided that more than anything she wanted to be a speaker herself.

"At first I would have to phone fifty prospects a day asking for a speaking assignment. Of those fifty people, about five would ask me to send material on myself. Of the five I might get only one speech—or none at all. Then, sometimes, after I had scheduled the speech, it would be cancelled! I made speeches to anyone for any price. I had to create ways to subsidize my income. During that time I didn't buy any new clothes. I had to study and work long hours. But I wanted to be a speaker badly enough that these sacrifices did not seem too great," she says. Jane did as anthropologist Joseph Campbell advises in *The Power of Myth*. She "followed her bliss," became successful, and overcame the frustrations and worries of working in a male-dominated institution.

Risking assertive behavior in a career may also mean changing your cognitive distortions and learning how to communicate. Dallas businesswoman Madeleine Hervey told us that her parents raised her to believe that a woman could do anything a man could. As a single parent who had to fight to get credit on her own, she saw that it was society that made it more difficult for women to do what men did, not necessarily women themselves. When she decided, in her thirties, to get her MBA, she discovered a new gender-related problem.

"I was the only woman in the class and the men really put me down. Whenever I spoke out in class, they made comments to let me know how stupid I was," she said. "I was so miserable that I almost dropped out." Then her mother gave her some good advice in the form of a needlepoint hanging which said in Latin, "Don't let the bastards get you down." Madeleine persevered. Once when a fellow student jokingly called her a "fluffhead," she faced him and said, "You're being rude and I don't like it." He backed off and so did the other students. Eventually these men became her friends.

At the end of the course her professor admitted that he had disapproved of the way the men bullied her.

"Why didn't you stop them?" she asked.

"Because you had to learn how to handle it yourself," he replied. Madeleine, who went on to become the owner of the Consider It Done shopping service in Dallas, discovered that learning to be assertive in the business world was an important part of her education.

If you need to make a career change, write down your action steps. You might:

- Take aptitude tests available from psychologists and employment agencies to see where your talents lie before making a change
- Talk to people who work in the fields that interest you to learn about opportunities
- Try to find a mentor by volunteering your services in professional organizations and clubs
- Write down your goals and start working on them

LETTING GO OF CAREER PROBLEMS

Lydia told her focus group about an experience in which letting go of career problems was the only viable alternative. "Two years ago my advertising and public relations business was a big success. Then the whole city suffered a recession, and the companies hurt the worst were my clients. My business disappeared overnight. I had to shut down my office and pay a penalty on my five-year lease. I had to lay off employees. I even had to move home with my parents. On the verge of a nervous breakdown, I started taking time for myself. I joined a support group, read books, talked with spiritual friends, and took a quantum leap of faith. I couldn't change what was going on around me, but I could change myself. I began to see that I had had too much of my emotional self invested in my career," Lydia said.

When career problems are beyond your control, a solution may be to let go, live in the present moment, and give up unrealistic expectations as Lydia did. Use the visualizing techniques of the Fifth SKILL Tool to do this. Forgive others and yourself.

"After going through this crisis, I now know that I am not my business or my financial success," Lydia said. "I am just myself, and I am okay. The strange thing is that when I gave up the control, the bills got paid and I kept my sanity. Going through this crisis has made me a stronger person."

Letting go is only one of the tools that may help you change your financial and career concerns into pearl worries. We hope that you will use them all to good benefit.

CHAPTER 12

◆ ◆ ◆

Getting Off the Relationship Worry-Go-Round

"When I was a little girl," said Marcia, a bank vice-president, "my parents told me I was just as smart as my brother. They encouraged me to compete in school activities and told me I could have a successful career, and I did. But they didn't tell me how to have a successful relationship. The role model my mother presented was to abdicate to my father in everything. In return, he did what he considered was best for her. That doesn't jell in today's world, and so my marriage is a mess. My husband and I can't communicate about anything that matters without fighting. I worry all the time about whether he's having an affair."

Though Marcia was a financial success, she felt like a failure in relating to men, as did many others in our focus groups. The relationship issues listed here were among the most frequent worries of the women to whom we spoke:

- Not being able to find a satisfactory relationship
- Inability to find happiness within a relationship
- Continuing a relationship after it became harmful
- Repeating the same mistakes in choosing new relationships

WHY WOMEN WORRY
ABOUT RELATIONSHIPS

"It's hard *not* to worry when you hear that women over thirty have little opportunity to marry and that 50 percent of all marriages end in divorce," said Maddie. "Without a man I feel like half a person. With one, I feel a loss of freedom and disappointment that I am not as happy as I expected to be."

Without realizing it, Maddie is expressing her neediness. If she doesn't have a man who "makes" her feel good about herself, the relationship is a failure. And she doesn't feel like a whole person if she is single. In *The Life Plus Program for Getting Unstuck*, we defined a healthy relationship as two or more people who have unconditional love for each other. That means that they are mutually committed to helping each other be all that they can be; that they share feelings honestly and accept the other person, even though he or she is less than perfect. In unhealthy relationships, partners are committed to fulfilling their own needs rather than to helping each other.

After Jane was divorced, she felt needy. "I worried about what would happen if I had to spend my life alone. I worried about what others would think if I didn't have a date. I worried about getting older and not being able to attract a man. I had a lot of fear of loneliness," she said. After she went through extensive therapy, she was able to accept her own strengths and weaknesses.

"I discovered that no other living human being could fill me with love. It had to come from a place of fullness that spilled over," she said. We believe that John Paul Zahody best describes the process of becoming serene with yourself in his inspirational book, *The Secret of Staying Together*. According to Zahody, the first step in finding and keeping a loving and supportive relationship is to learn personal integrity. You must first become aware of your ideal before you can express it in the activity of your lives.

When we met Zahody before our marriage he told us, "Your ability to recognize the integrity of true commitment in yourself and in your partner comes directly from your own daily practice of integrity—from the quality of commitment to honesty, fairness, consistency, and excellence of performance that prevails in your personal affairs."

Our SKILL Tools can help you discern whether you are worrying about relationships because you have failed to meet your own needs. You can consider new alternatives, choose a goal, and risk new behavior that may solve your problem. If not, you can use the letting go tool and emerge a stronger, more secure person.

GOOD GUYS AND BAD GUYS

Jane once attended a seminar on relationships in which the leader asked everyone to look at a picture of a Vietnam jungle clearing and find five booby traps. Nearly everyone could find four, but the leader had to point out the fifth.

"How many of you saw the sniper with the gun in his hand?" he asked. No one had because the man was hiding behind a tree, almost obscured by shadows.

"If you had been in this jungle, you would have been dead within seconds, simply because you didn't see the danger," the therapist explained. Then he pointed out that many women are equally unwary in choosing relationships. They walk through mine-laden battlefields, believing they are perfectly safe because they think they have located all the booby traps, but they miss the most dangerous one of all—the man with the weapon. That is why some women continue to choose one alcoholic or abusive partner after another.

Our friend Mara, who has had three failed marriages, worries about whether her future relationships will be as devastating as those of the past. All her husbands had seemed like good choices before marriage. They were handsome men with better-than-average incomes who liked to party. After marriage, they all had affairs—and venereal disease. Each complained that she was demanding and self-centered. She talked on the phone too much and sometimes went to bed too early!

"If I had been a 'better wife,' would I have been able to save my marriage?" Mara asks. Mara is right to ask herself what part she played in the failure of her marriages, but wrong to take on the guilt of not being a good wife. If Mara had had higher self-esteem and better knowledge of how to communicate the ideals that are really important to her, she would have spotted the danger signals before she became deeply involved with these men. She would have chosen a man without a gun in his hand!

If you are afraid that you will not be able to find a satisfactory relationship, or if a current relationship is causing you anxiety, use the First SKILL Tool to seek the real reason for your worries. Ask yourself the following questions:

• *Are your worries psychosocial?* Are you relating to men through a sense of neediness? Do you need this man to make you acceptable in a couple-oriented society? Do you expect his good looks, money, know-how, or prestige to make you feel better about yourself? Margo told her focus group how her neediness had soured a relationship which she expected to blossom. "Al and I had what you might call a telephone romance for several months. We started out talking to each other as friends. As we shared more and more of our deeper thoughts, I really began to care about him. Then one night he suggested we go to the Bahamas together. I had never even had a single date with him, but I said yes. While we were there, I was so happy with him that I told him I thought he was the man of my life. Then he backed away. After we got home, he said, 'I'll be seeing you,' and he never called again," she said. Because of her need to have a man care for her, Margo plunged from a telephone conversation into intimacy. Not only did she lose the romantic relationship, but she lost a friend as well.

Look at the childhood experiences you wrote in your journal after reading chapter 2. Are any of these at the root of feeling helpless, dependent, or passive when you are with men? If so, set a goal to increase your feeling of self-worth so that you will be able to share gifts with a love partner rather than attempt to fill your needs.

• *Are your worries instinctive?* In a relationship, do you try to nurture your mate by doing things that he could (and should) do for himself, rescuing him from mistakes that he needs to face, and generally acting as a mother to him? Do you acquiesce to his wish to be the "head of the house" even though the decisions he makes are faulty? If you feel you are being abused, verbally or physically, your nurturing instincts may be out of control. In her revealing book, *Woman's Reality*, psychotherapist Anne Wilson Schaef tells of a client who went to such extremes to mother her husband that she cut up his meat for him as if he were a child. Once, when this couple was invited to dinner by the boss, she forgot where she was and started cutting up his steak. The incident was so embarrassing that they decided to seek counseling.

Examine the childhood incidents you wrote about after reading chapter 3. Ask yourself whether these incidents cause you to overuse your nurturing instincts so that they become, in effect, a form of codependency for your partner's bad habits. If so, set a goal to become more assertive.

• *Are your worries societal?* Are you confused about your responsibilities in a relationship in light of the changing role of women? Are your expectations realistic that the man in your relationship will share equally in housekeeping and child-rearing duties? Are you so tired from working that you don't have the time or energy for a satisfactory sex life? Since your husband works daily with so many attractive women, do you worry that he will become involved in an affair?

Schaef also describes the societal influences she has discovered through her years of counseling both sexes. Women, she says must function in what she terms the White Male System. Men hold all the power and believe that the way they think, behave, and relate is the only acceptable way. In the White Male System's "Perfect Marriage," the man outwardly functions as the parent of the wife. While he makes all the decisions and handles the money, she boosts his ego by remaining childlike and allowing him to care for her. Behind closed doors, however, the roles are reversed. The wife takes the position of the mother who must feed, clothe, and pick up after her childlike husband.

The Female System, in contrast, sees time as a process or series of passages rather than what the numbers on a clock measure, relationships as more important than self or work, intimacy as sharing and discussing lives rather than being physically close, and love as a flow of energy rather than a series of rituals. Unfortunately, the Female System has been ineffectual because of influence by the White Male System: Women believe something is inherently wrong with them because being women, they don't think, act, and behave as men do. Women try to compensate for these inadequacies by being very good or by being completely fair, only to be taken advantage of by the White Male System.

Women are in a catch-22 position in relationships. If they live by the rules of the Female System, men—who hold much of the power in our culture—tell them they are misfits. If they try to live by the rules of the White Male System, men may resent them and women may then feel a sense of unworthiness and a loss of self-esteem. In today's world where a woman works every bit as hard as a man does (while being paid less) and has just as little time for housework and familial responsibilities, relationships will undoubtedly suffer. We wait for a co-equal, genderless system to evolve.

We believe that these societal attitudes multiply the worries involved in relationships. Women may not be able to reverse the White Male System singlehandedly, but they can change their *own* relationships. They can learn to be assertive and decisive while developing a Female System that includes a sense of self-worth. If you feel better about yourself, you will deal with relationship problems more directly. You also will be better equipped to give and receive the love between equals that you seek from a man.

If you feel incapable of solving relationship problems because of the male advantage, set a goal to improve your problem-solving and decision-making skills. For instance, you can learn to communicate your ideas, needs, and wishes more clearly. You can decide to base decisions on what is good for you rather than excluding your own needs.

• *Are your worries physiological?* Do hormonal fluctuations or PMS sometimes cause you to overreact to the stresses in relationships? If so, seek medical attention to pinpoint and correct the problem.

It is best if you can ask yourself these questions before you become involved in a relationship. Then you can learn the skills that will make it possible to attract a compatible partner who supports your desire to grow. However, since it is hard to foresee differences that may cause problems with another person, issues may crop up that you had not expected. Don't put yourself down because you don't have the perfect relationship. Think of a relationship as constantly changing and as a great learning opportunity. If you are already in a relationship that is causing you to worry, the questions below may help you set goals for fulfilling your own needs. For instance, you can set a goal to read a book or take a course to improve your self-esteem so that you won't have to depend on having a good-looking, wealthy, or prestigious man to feel worthy. When you recognize the good in yourself, you may lessen the stress in your relationships.

As you look at yourself, however, remember Schaef's theory about the White Male System: Many women try to solve their relationship problems by becoming super good and super fair. When you are looking at the real reasons for your worry, avoid playing a form of "My Fault" and taking responsibility for your partner's character flaws. If you can't tell whether you are wearing the black or the white hat in the relationship, or if it seems that both of you are wearing gray, then ask yourself the following questions:

1. *Who owns the problem?* If your partner is irresponsible about money and overspends the budget, the problem is his, not yours. If you are in an emotional turmoil because you feel you don't have enough money, the problem may be yours.

2. *Who is affected by the problem?* Whether the problem is that your partner is irresponsible or that you can't adjust to your income, you and your partner are both affected. Identify your feelings. Are you angry, sad, hurt, confused?

3. *What do you want to do about the problem?* At this point you can begin to brainstorm and plan how to communicate your feelings, wants, and needs assertively. See chapter 9 to plan your strategy for communicating assertively.

USING THE SKILL TOOLS TO FIND A SATISFACTORY RELATIONSHIP

When Marianne brainstormed some solutions to her worry of not being able to find a mate, she selected the "I'm Not Willing" tool. Divorced for five years, Marianne at thirty-eight felt pressured by her parents' and friends' theme song: "You're being too particular about your men."

"I took a good, hard look at the way I felt when I was married to a man who kept putting me down. I decided I was much better off single than in a similar relationship again; and the only kind of men I met seemed to be complete losers. I learned to tell myself, 'I'm not willing to date someone who is only out for sex, nor am I willing to date just to find a man' " she said. Marianne did not spend her time moping alone, however. She took some time to think about the qualities she wanted in a mate (*Know your alternatives*.). She wanted someone who was loving and accepting, who could communicate his feelings, and who enjoyed good music. She wrote down her wishes, and then made sure she could offer the same qualities to a man in return. She even took a course in assertive communication so that she would be able to express feelings without being aggressive (*Let yourself risk*.). She imaged the kind of man she wanted to meet and affirmed that she was going to meet him. She *let go* of any unrealistic expectations she had of transforming the men, whom she already knew as frogs, into princes. After using the SKILL Tools, Marianne did meet her prince—one who was committed to sharing the duties of their "kingdom" equally. And she feels self-confident enough to maintain this well-balanced relationship.

If you are trying to find a compatible partner, divide a sheet of paper into two columns. Write down the requirements you expect in a man in the first column. For instance, you might write that your ideal partner must:

• Have a sense of humor
• Have a better-than-average salary
• Be willing to share household duties
• Enjoy classical music

Then write down your assets in the other column. Are the two columns in balance? Do you have as much to bring to the relationship as you expect from the man? Perhaps you are in balance except that your sense of humor is not what it should be. If not, set your goal to improve your sense of humor. Use visualizations and affirmations to gain the help of your unconscious in making changes— and in bringing the man you want into your acquaintance. See yourself enjoying a symphony concert with a man beside you whose eyes shine with love for you. Picture yourself with friends who introduce you to the perfect man. Use positive expectancy that there is such a man for you.

One night as we were having dinner in a restaurant, we could not help noticing a woman who sat alone at the next table. She looked so miserable and unhappy that we commented on how unattractive she was. Then a man whom she obviously knew walked up and asked if he could join her. As he did so, her face lit up. She changed from gargoyle to beauty queen in an instant. Suddenly, she had the kind of inner joy and radiance that could have attracted almost any man.

How do you get this kind of radiance if you don't already have it? First, give yourself permission to fill your needs that don't concern a man. When you are content with yourself, then visualize yourself looking calm, confident, and happy, as the man of your dreams walks to you. Set a goal to be able to express your self-contentment and joyful expectancy. Practice smiling at the people you meet during the day. Tell others about the things in your life that you find enjoyable. Write out how you will act *as if* you are happy even on days when you're feeling lonely. Write down an "atta girl" on your goal sheet when you are successful. We think that you'll find the same radiance that shone forth from the woman in the restaurant—just waiting to be invited out!

USING THE SKILL TOOLS TO KEEP A GOOD RELATIONSHIP HEALTHY

Focus group members who were married or in a relationship told us that some of their biggest worries revolved around the fear of losing the relationship.

"Mark has a habit of telling me, 'Oh, don't be silly,' whenever I express how I feel about myself or even when we discuss a news story about which I have an opinion that is different from his," Sandi told her focus group. "I don't say anything to defend myself, but I really get angry about it. We usually end up not speaking. Then I start imagining that the reason he is giving me the silent treatment is because he is having an affair. He could easily be involved with one of the young, attractive female buyers with whom he travels to the wholesale markets. My imagination works like an X-rated movie. I see him in bed having sex with one or the other of them. Then I get even angrier, but I worry too. I'm afraid he'll leave me. The result is that when he wants to have sex with me, I'm too upset to enjoy it. I fake it because I'm afraid to talk to him about how I feel for fear that he really would get angry and leave me."

Sandi is involved in a process that psychologists call "chaining." She represses her anger over Mark's frequent "Don't be silly," statements, but it doesn't go away. It only generates other worries— first, about whether Mark is having an affair, then about whether he will leave her. With all her unexpressed anger, fear, and worry, it is not surprising that Sandi is unable to enjoy sex. Then she worries about whether she is frigid.

If Sandi uses the First SKILL Tool to seek the real reason for all her relationship worries, she will see that it starts with her anger over being put down. Such anger, says Jim Wilson, is often a sign of having no control over the situation. If a woman is not willing either to leave such situations or make changes in herself, she reinforces a feeling of helplessness.

"You can't change someone else, but you can learn assertive communication in order to ventilate the anger," Jim says. "You can create a plan to develop your feelings of self-esteem, starting with small things. For example, take up body building or some other physical activity, or take college courses. If you are not already working, get a part-time job. When you begin to change your responses to the person with whom you are angry, then he may start treating you differently too. If you begin to do things that support yourself and reinforce your positive feelings about your-self, then you won't tend to buy into put-downs as much any more."

We agree that these are good alternatives to pursue. To learn to speak up for yourself and increase your self-esteem, take a stimulating course, join a support group, or read some inspiring books. We recommend *Self-Esteem* by Matthew McKay, Ph.D., and Patrick Fanning, and *Don't Say Yes When You Want to Say No,* by Herbert Fensterheim, Ph.D., and Jean Baer. In addition, use the Fourth

SKILL Tool and take some risks. Plan how you will change your thoughts, words, and actions regarding the problem. Consider what part the list of Top Ten Cognitive Distortions in chapter 9 plays in your thinking and reframe those thoughts. Consider what you want the other person to do. Then write out your plan of action for communicating what you think, feel, and want.

For instance, Sandi can quickly see that she is feeling angry and hurt. "You're a second-class citizen," her inner critic tells her when Mark puts her down. She should write down these feelings and then assess the validity of these thoughts about herself. By looking at the list of Top Ten Cognitive Distortions, Sandi can see that she really is not a "second-class citizen," but that she is simply experiencing rejectionitis. She is so hurt and angry about the put-down that she thinks in negative focus terms and starts chaining worries about Mark's faithlessness. Knowing this, she can reframe these distortions by writing, "When Mark calls me silly, it does not mean that I lack intelligence. It only means that he has a problem accepting the fact that I have my own opinions. I know that I am plenty smart, so I don't have to take what he is dishing out." Sandi also can reframe her negative focus worries that Mark is having an affair by telling herself, "Just because Mark has a bad habit of putting me down doesn't mean that he feels no love for me. I have plenty of good qualities that appeal to Mark."

After she has determined what she is feeling and thinking, Sandi can write out a plan of action for communicating to Mark what she wants him to do. In private she will practice telling him, "When you call me silly, I feel like a second-class citizen. I feel so hurt and angry that I can't love you as I would like. I want you to stop calling me silly." To make the role-playing even more effective, Sandi can create a visualization of herself saying these words in a calm manner while Mark listens and responds calmly. She can also use the Fifth SKILL Tool to forgive Mark for his past mistakes and to let go of the worry that he will be angry at her for what she says.

If Sandi actually risks communicating to Mark in this way, he may agree to stop calling her silly. Even if he does not, she will begin breaking the self-destructive habit of chaining worries, because she has affirmed herself. As she continues to communicate assertively, Sandi may gain enough self-confidence to tell Mark her feelings, thoughts, and wishes regarding their sexual relationship.

Assertiveness means not only asking a person to stop actions that bother you. As Dr. Herbert Fensterheim points out in *Don't Say Yes When You Want to Say No*, it also includes communicating positive feelings and requests to your partner. You can do this by writing out:

- I like _____ (what you said).
- I like _____ (what you did).
- I want you to _____ (give me more positive attention).

After you practice expressing these feelings in private, try them out on your mate. Using a positive framework is an especially constructive way to communicate your sexual desires.

You may not always get what you ask for when you communicate assertively, but at least you will have expressed your own needs. You will also know where you stand with the other person. While this knowledge may be scary, in the long run it will help you to grow. Regardless of the outcome, your self-esteem will increase and you will be better able to handle future relationship problems.

USING THE SKILL TOOLS TO LET GO OF A HARMFUL RELATIONSHIP

We are not saying that you can end *all* of your relationship worries by using the SKILL Tools. When two people of different tastes, temperaments, and goals come together, some stress is inevitable. We are saying, however, that you can change a vicious cycle of worry to pearl worry by learning and growing and seeing whether your partner is willing to do the same. We are also saying that sometimes the best answer to relationship worries is to let go of the relationship.

"I did all the things that you are talking about for sixteen years," Melanie told her focus group. "I went to counselors, I read books, I communicated in 'I feel' statements, but the truth is that we were not growing at the same rate. We didn't communicate on the same level. I liked light, he liked dark. I liked to party, play, laugh, and talk about things that mattered with other people. He wanted to sit and watch TV. Besides that, he would fly into a rage if I didn't follow every rule he set out, and though I tried very hard to please him, he always changed the rules in the middle of the game. Being married to him for so long wasn't good for me. What was wrong with me to stay with him for so long?"

Many women stay in destructive relationships because of worry. "What will people think if I get a divorce?" "How can I make it without a man?" "How can I handle my rage, loneliness, hurt?" "What if no one else wants me?" Even though your current relationship may be as incomplete as a jigsaw puzzle with two missing pieces, you may cling to it because of these worries. By denying that anything is wrong with the relationship, you may endure more unhappiness than if you take your courage in both hands and leave your mate.

In their helpful book, *Loveshock*, Stephen Gullo, Ph.D. and Connie Church say that when you let go of a love relationship you may react like a shell-shocked soldier. First you go through a state of shock that prevents you from sleeping, concentrating, or feeling deep emotion for others. This numb stage is followed by periods of grief, blaming, resignation (saying good-bye), and finally resolution and rebuilding. Along the way you may experience nausea, loss of appetite, depression, and crying jags, and above all, an emptiness deep inside. It is as if you have lost part of yourself.

Both of us know from firsthand experience the pain of going through a divorce. We also recognize the gifts we have received because of the changes we made in response to that pain. In order to survive loveshock, Jane risked going through extensive therapy which brought about a transformation in the way she felt about herself, men, her career, and her whole life. Bob felt that he grew a great deal after his divorce. Only after our divorces did either of us find Life Plus. We believe that the SKILL Tools can help you survive loveshock too.

Begin by seeking the real reason for your worry about ending the relationship. Is it fear of what others might think? Fear of being a failure? Fear of finding a relationship that demands the best you can offer? Fear of never finding a good relationship? These psychosocial reasons for worry stem from your perception that while others are permitted to make mistakes, you aren't. On a sheet of paper, use the "So what?" Technique.

"So what if my relationship ended?"
"No one in my family has ever gotten a divorce. Everyone else seems to be able to 'hold onto a man,' but I can't."
"So what?"
"I don't like feeling like a failure."
"So what?"
"So I'll be especially good to myself while I'm going through loveshock."

Now write out your cognitive distortions. Remind yourself that every year half as many people divorce as marry, so you are not a pariah. Recognize when you are thinking in perfectionistic, negative terms. Reframe your cognitions by writing, "I am a loving person who deserves happiness," and "It is okay for me to be human and make mistakes." Visualize and affirm these truths.

Are your worries instinctive? Do you feel that you are only half a person without a man who will love you in return for your care? Monica told her focus group, "It's been one-and-a-half years since my divorce, and I just don't want to do anything. I don't want to travel, I don't want a lot of money. I don't even want a mate. I worry a lot because I don't seem normal. It's bad not to have dreams." Monica does not realize that she is describing a typical loveshock reaction. It may take her a long time to reach a state of resolution and rebuilding. She needs to give herself permission to feel the way she feels and to be patient and loving toward herself. If she doesn't feel like dating yet, she doesn't have to push herself to do it. Meanwhile, she can nurture herself.

If you are having trouble adjusting to single status, set a goal to fulfill your needs on your own. Realize that while a relationship can fulfill the need for companionship, only you can make yourself feel good about yourself. Using the Third SKILL Tool, imagine yourself feeling good about yourself. Image yourself enjoying your skills, talents, friends, and accomplishments as a single person.

Affirm that you are a person of worth who deserves happiness. Whenever Mr. Negative tells you you are a half-person, affirm that you are perfectly happy and can fill your own needs.

Are your worries societal? Are you afraid that you can't make it financially or socially without a man? If so, you may need to develop problem-solving skills so that you are able to deal with life's ups and downs. Before you leave a relationship, plan ahead. It is all too true that many men take advantage of women financially in a divorce. When Jane was on the verge of a divorce, she read Lynette Triere's helpful book, *Learning to Leave*. It advised listing insurance policies, stock holdings, and other assets—even writing down the serial numbers for autos and making photostats of important documents so you would know ahead of time what kind of settlement you should get.

"When you are in an emotional state, it is hard to think clearly about what you will need financially and how to protect yourself," says Jane. "Yet doing so may make all the difference in how easily you can adjust afterward."

Are your worries caused by physiological problems? You may feel low because the stress of loveshock is generating depression. To overcome this, use the Third SKILL Tool's relaxation techniques. Listen to soothing music; take up a spirit-nourishing hobby like needlepoint, painting, or playing the piano to take you out of your worries. Jogging and other aerobic activities will cause your body to generate endorphins, the body's natural tranquilizers, which will help you feel better. If deep sadness persists, you may find comfort in a support group or from some professional counseling.

TAKING STEPS

We think that the example of Kay Woodruff Fanning, former editor of the *Christian Science Monitor*, shows the importance of letting go of the feeling of failure when a relationship dissolves. It also shows that working through such an experience holds its own rewards. Married to multimillionaire husband Marshall Field IV for thirteen years, Kay found nothing but unhappiness as a "society wife," according to her inspiring story in the book, *Take Two*, by Jo Brans. As Brans tells it, while her husband managed a publishing empire that included the *Chicago Sun-Times*, the *Chicago Daily News*, and Simon & Schuster, Kay was expected to relinquish any hope of having her own career and to focus instead on raising children and entertaining guests. Her marriage ended, but Kay, it seemed, understood that positive things could result from painful events.

"I'm not about to say that it wouldn't be absolutely wonderful to find the right career and the right husband right out of college and to go forward from there. But I do think that a certain amount of turmoil and trouble probably helps us grow a little. When things work too easily, maybe one doesn't grow as much," she was quoted as saying.

Grow Kay did. She gave up cigarettes, tranquilizers, and sleeping pills and moved to Alaska. Although she had never worked, she got a job with the *Anchorage Daily News* as a librarian. After three years of developing her own talents, she married Larry Fanning, a seasoned newspaperman. The two bought the *Anchorage Daily News*, and with it supported unpopular ecological stands for four years until Larry died. "I was very deeply in love with Larry," she says in the book. "We were quite wonderful together. He was everything to me." Continuing alone, she eventually took the demanding job of editor of the *Christian Science Monitor*.

As it was for Kay Fanning, the end of one relationship can open the window of opportunity for growth that will make possible a successful relationship later on. By using the SKILL Tools to get at the root cause of relationship worries, you will be better prepared to live the Life Plus way as a single person or with the man you love.

CHAPTER 13

♦ ◆ ♦

Using the SKILL Tools to Resolve Worries over Children

"When my four-year-old runs into the street without looking for oncoming cars, I go out of my mind with worry," Melinda told her focus group. "I've tried telling him that he might get run over, but it hasn't done any good, so I've started spanking him—and that makes me worry even more. Some parenting books say you should spank, but others say that spanking causes shame and guilt that can scar children for life. I don't want to harm my son psychologically, but I don't want him to get run over, either."

Michelle's parenting problem involves her ten-year-old daughter, who claims that her teacher is picking on her in class. "If I call for a conference and complain to the teacher, will I be overprotecting my daughter? If I don't, will she think that I don't love her? I can't sleep at night for thinking about this," she said.

Myra is panicky because her seventeen-year-old now has his driver's license, a part-time job, and his own car. "He's so impulsive that I'd like to limit his driving to the neighborhood, but it's his car. I don't feel I have any control, and I'm worried sick that I'll get a phone call telling me he's had a wreck and is hospitalized or even dead," she told the focus group.

Most mothers are all too aware that every year hundreds of children are run over, thousands drop out of school, and teenage driving accidents kill hundreds more. Newscasts tell of the increasing numbers of adolescent suicides. Drug dealers lurk in the best of schools. Missing children stare out at us from photos on milk carton labels. Mothers feel responsible for protecting their children from these tragedies, yet they are not sure what they should do. When they consult parenting experts, they often receive conflicting advice. So it's easy for mothers to fall prey to worry; in their minds, if they just worry enough, all those bad things won't happen!

The worry themes that surfaced most often among mothers in our focus groups revolved around not knowing how to:

- Discipline without harming children emotionally
- Protect children from poor health and accidents
- Keep children away from drugs, alcohol, sex, and teenagers who exert a bad influence
- Motivate children to do well in school
- Be a "good enough" mother

Does worry help to achieve these goals? Most women seem to realize that worry helps out when it leads to changed behavior and alternate ways of doing things. But when worry keeps you awake at three o'clock in the morning because things aren't changing, it's hard to fight it off, even when you know it is counterproductive.

"Worrying is a part of parenting," said Millie, a sixty-two-year-old mother of four. "If you are a mother, you want to guide your children, but you never know for sure exactly what they are doing. You want them to become independent and productive adults, and you feel sole responsibility for helping them become that way. Now that my children are grown, I realize that you have to separate your desire that your children have good and happy lives from worrying about it, because worry is destructive."

We believe that Millie is right when she says that good parents will want to protect their infants from sickness, safety hazards, and the abuse of others. We also agree that worry itself is never productive. In addition to the self-destructiveness of worrying (since you serve as a role model that your children will emulate). your worry triggers feelings of poor self-esteem in your child. Why? The more frequently you communicate to your children that you are on the worry-go-round, the more likely your children will grow up to become anxious, timid, and afraid to risk in what they come to see as a danger-fraught world.

In his book, *A Good Enough Parent*, the late child psychologist Dr. Bruno Bettelheim says, "Parental anxiety makes life very difficult for parent and child, since the child responds to the anxiety of the parents with even more severe anxiety, and then their anxieties aggravate each other. . . . The child responds to whatever aroused the parent's anxiety as if it were truly a world-shattering event. The reason for this is that a child's shaky security depends, as he well knows, not on his abilities to protect himself, but on the goodwill of others; it is borrowed from the security of his parents. When they suddenly seem unable to cope, he loses whatever small measure of security he has had."

Another focus group member said, "I can't imagine that parents will ever reach a point where they don't worry about their children. I just hope we learn how to turn most worry into positive, fruitful concern rather than that shapeless, nameless worry that produces anxiety in other people whenever they are around it."

If your aim is to be a good mother, you will be better able to deal with dangers and problems if you don't get stuck on the worry-go-round. If you are confident in the way you relate to your children, you will not cause them to become timid and anxious. While we cannot tell you which style of parenting is best for you and your children, our SKILL Tools can help you eliminate some of the worry that can get in the way of your relationship with your children.

THE PATHWAYS TO WORRY OVER CHILDREN

Use the First SKILL Tool to investigate the reasons for your worry:

• *Are your worries psychosocial?* Do you worry about your children because your mother worried about you? "One of the biggest worries my mother had was that something bad might happen to the children," Naomi told Bob after reading *Anxiety and Panic Attacks*. "After I had an auto accident at fifteen, she worried even more. Now I find I'm doing the same thing with my children." Housebound with agoraphobia, Naomi could see that she was modeling fearful, anxious behavior to her children. When she started going to an alpha state in order to stave off panic attacks, she discovered that she could also program herself to feel less anxious about her children being in an accident. When she stopped reacting to her children in a fearful way, she discovered that they became less timid and more able to assess risks objectively.

Another clue that you may be on the Psychosocial Path to Worry is perceiving yourself as being somehow unworthy of expressing your true feelings. For instance, do you feel insecure about setting limits for your children? Do you find that it is hard to tell your children that you love them? Do you push your children to accomplish things you always wanted to do but which don't interest them? Do you feel that others are judging you on the basis of whether your child is a "success" or not?

If you answered yes to these questions, give yourself permission to reflect on what you really want for your children. Remember that your children will reflect your demeanor back to you: if you express love, so will they. Use the Fourth SKILL Tool to risk identifying your feelings, communicating, and suggesting alternatives. Listen and respond to what your children say to you. By nurturing yourself and increasing your self-esteem, you will gain the confidence you need to risk being "real" with your children, and maybe they'll feel safe to reveal *their* deepest wishes and dreams to you in return. When you open up, they open up (since you are their model). You will be able to give them the positive attention they need to grow into the persons they were meant to be.

• *Are your worries instinctive?* When you give birth, you have the instinctive urge to feed, nurture, love, and protect your infant from danger. As your child grows, however, your task becomes one of gradually letting go of control. You need to allow your child to take the consequences of his or her actions, good or bad, in order to learn a sense of responsibility. Do you know how to draw the line between rescuing your children from real danger and letting them suffer the consequences of immature actions? Can you permit your children to risk and make a mistake?

Nan worried frantically when her eight- and ten-year-olds got bad marks on their report cards for arriving late at school. "I was afraid they would learn to hate school. I lay awake at night picturing them as dropouts by the time they were fifteen. I just couldn't let that happen, because I was their mother and I was responsible for them," she said. Nan started waking her children earlier and earlier. She nagged and yelled at them to hurry, but somehow they always seemed to dawdle just long enough to miss the last bell. Then a wise teacher told Nan to buy her children an alarm clock and let them wake themselves. The first week, the children overslept and dawdled. They arrived at school later than ever. Every day that week they received a detention, but Nan forced herself not to react. On the mornings when the alarm went off and Nan heard no sounds from the children's bedrooms, she restrained herself from waking them. She kept calm by using our relaxation and letting go techniques. She would go to an alpha state and visualize herself in her secret resting place while affirming that she was a worthy person. She also realized that she didn't have to think in "My Fault" terms: She was not the only one responsible for her children getting to school on time.

When the children complained about the detentions, she refused to point out that it was all their own fault. She simply agreed that it was too bad that they had to miss out on the after-school soccer game. By the second week, the children understood that their mother was not going to rescue them. They began to get out of bed when their alarm went off. They started arriving at school on time. Nan no longer worried because she had nothing to worry about!

Consider whether you might be following the Instinctive Path to Worry by holding on to problems that belong to your children rather than to you. Are you overprotecting your children from the minor bumps, bruises, and detentions that will help them grow? We are certainly not advocating neglect, but we hope you will identify which issues you yourself must control in order to safeguard your child and which you should let your children handle, and letting go of the latter by consulting with teachers you trust, school counselors, parents you admire, or qualified therapists. If you don't stop shielding your children from their responsibilities when they are young, you may still be rescuing your children when they are older and worrying as much as ever. To get off this path, make goals to increase your self-esteem. When you feel good about yourself, you will not have to depend on filling your children's needs to find your own identity.

• *Are your worries societal?* Are you anxious about your child's becoming involved with drugs, alcohol, unsafe sex, or crime? These are real dangers that require you to be assertive and to develop problem-solving skills. When you have done your best, by pointing out the dangers and modeling appropriate behavior, set your goal to eliminate ceaseless worry which is destructive to you and to your children.

Dr. Rege Stewart, a psychiatrist at the University of Texas Southwestern Medical School, says that parents who are worried about problems beyond their control should first take active steps to help their teenagers and then accept the fact that teenagers are responsible for their own actions.

"If your teenagers have problems, recognize them and get adequate professional help. Express your concern to them. Share with them why you are concerned and what your fears are. For instance, if your teenagers are using drugs, tell them that it is not in their best interests because of all the negative consequences of drug use. You care a great deal about them, and you don't want them to get hurt but if they insist on getting hurt, there's no way you can protect them from it. It's their responsibility, and they have to live with the consequences of their actions. Then accept it. This is easily said; it's much harder to execute when you are the mother or father who deeply cares about your child's future. However, if you don't accept it, you can get yourself into deep depression over something you can't control."

• *Are your worries physiological?* Do you have the stamina it takes to deal with the physical challenges of caring for children? Are you so tired all the time that you tend to fall into the trap of worry rather than take action? Do you worry more than you should because hormonal fluctuations put you in a blue mood?

As a single parent with a demanding job, Natalie dreaded picking up her children from the day-care center. "I was so tired that I wanted only to lie down and rest. Instead, the children always started badgering me for attention. Then I worried about why the kids wouldn't eat supper, why they wouldn't go to bed on time, why their noses ran, and whether they would get sick and I would have to miss work to take care of them. Every month while I was experiencing PMS, I told myself that I was a terrible mother. I was to blame for everything that was wrong with them," she said.

Natalie was fortunate that the day-care center remained open long enough that she could leave her children there for an extra half hour while she took a few minutes of quiet time for herself. She also asked for and followed her doctor's advice on how to deal with PMS and took extra good care of herself on those days. When she felt better, the worries looked smaller, and she could better enjoy her children too.

FORGING AHEAD VERSUS LETTING GO

By now you can see that the solutions to worries about children involve both problem-solving and letting go. When you use the Second SKILL Tool to look for alternatives, brainstorm creative ways to solve problems and let go. On a sheet of paper write, "I am worried that my child _____." (Describe disturbing actions.) Note whether you write in the present or future tense. If the action is going on in the present moment, you might say something like, "I am worried because my daughter sucks her thumb," or "My son runs around with friends I don't like." For present-day situations you take action. Brainstorm some possible solutions and then select the best.

To follow the examples, you might read what experts advise about thumb-sucking and follow their suggestions, or you might seek professional help. You could ask your daughter to stop sucking her thumb and remind her that if she does, her hands are not free to play with her toys. As for your son, you might tell him why you feel his friends make unwise decisions or take unnecessary risks. Ask his school counselor and teachers how he is getting along to see if he has a problem. You could stock your refrigerator with snacks to attract your son and his friends to your home, where you will be in a position to support positive activities.

As you deal with your children's present-moment problems, remember to avoid worry partners who will undermine your determination to risk action rather than fall back into worry. When Mr. Negative calls, refuse to speak with him! Visualize yourself speaking calmly with your children about the things they are doing that you don't like. See them responding to you in a positive way. Affirm that you are perfectly capable of communicating with your children and of changing your own behavior.

Now let us look at the techniques you can use when you are worrying about the future. If you write, "I am afraid that my daughter will have an overbite if she does not stop sucking her thumb," or "I am afraid that my son's friends will push him into vandalism," you are describing an event that has not yet happened. Recognize that when the word *will* is used, you are not living in the present moment. You are predicting catastrophes. You are thinking in white-is-black terms, looking at neutral facts and creating negative conclusions. You are playing the "What If?" game. Recognize that you cannot change or control an event that has not yet happened. Your only alternative is to let go. You can do that by restructuring your futuristic statements.

You might write, "I have no way of knowing whether my daughter will have an overbite if she keeps on sucking her thumb. If she does, I can take her to an orthodontist." Or, "Even though I do not like my son's friends, it does not necessarily mean that he will get into vandalism. I am taking action to prevent him from doing that. I serve him better when I visualize good rather than bad things happening to him."

Whenever you catch yourself visualizing terrible scenarios, immediately draw a big red X over the scene in your mind. Then go to an alpha state, relax, and see the future as you want it to be. See your daughter playing happily without sucking her thumb. See your son choosing wholesome friends and enjoying them. See yourself remaining perfectly calm as you speak to him. Affirm that you *are* this way.

We like the distraction techniques used by our friend, Sheila Murray Bethal. Sheila, a wonderful speaker whose latest book is titled, *Making a Difference: The Twelve Qualities to Make You a Leader*, told us, "When I was a young mother raising children, I noticed how harmful worry was to women. I developed a daytime and a nighttime technique to deal with worry about my family and my business so that I wouldn't get into what I call the 'worry mode.' That's when you let some little thing that you ordinarily could shrug off turn into a mountain.

"My daytime technique is to tell myself, "I'll worry about it on Friday. Whenever a worry comes up during the week I tell myself I'm too busy to worry about it then, but I'll write it down. By Friday when I look at my list, I find that about 90 percent of my worries have disappeared. They just haven't happened. For the rest, I do spend a few moments worrying, but by Friday they don't seem to amount to much anyway. I don't waste more than ten minutes on them.

"My nighttime technique is based on the fact that you can't hold two thoughts at the same time. I repeat the Twenty-third Psalm and say the Lord's Prayer. Then I run through a list of blessings. For instance, my mother suffered a terrible stroke and she did not make much progress in rehabilitation. I consciously replaced my worry for her with the thought that it was a blessing that she now could use her left hand to feed herself, and that she could sit up by herself for a short while. It didn't take long to begin to feel peaceful and then to go to sleep."

WHAT TO DO WHEN THE OYSTER DOESN'T SEEM TO CONTAIN A PEARL

When we talk about letting go of worries, we recognize that sometimes devastating things happen to children: babies get leukemia, children are kidnapped or killed, adolescents commit suicide. Of course you will worry if your children are threatened by such possibilities. You will want to do everything you can to prevent these catastrophes, but worry won't have any preventive effect. You will especially want to let go of worry if some tragedy befalls your child.

When Jane was four years old and lying in the hospital near death from her burns, her mother, Rachel, kept punishing herself with "If Onlys." "Yes, I know that I was trying to protect Jane from getting polio by keeping her in the house and boiling eggs for her to color the day that she pulled the pot full of scalding water off the stove. But why did I not take the pot off the stove so that she couldn't get to it? When my neighbor came by, why didn't I tell her I couldn't talk to her because I had to watch Jane? Why didn't I get an egg for Jane when she asked for it instead of telling her to wait a minute?"

Jane's mother was so filled with guilt and anxiety that her doctor told her, "Rachel, get hold of yourself or you won't be able to take care of Jane." Rachel began to concentrate on building Jane's self-esteem rather than worrying that her mistake was going to ruin Jane's future. She learned to tell Jane that she was beautiful on the inside even when other children drew away from her ugly scars. Rachel never felt good about the accident, but by acting in a positive way rather than focusing on feelings of guilt, she tried to help Jane feel good about herself despite the tragic incident. This was the kind of nurturing mother Jane needed most—not one distracted by guilt and worry.

How hard it is to give up the "If Onlys"! Jane once taught school with a woman who finally gave birth to a much-wanted baby daughter. Five years and three miscarriages later, Neva had a second baby girl. Neva was thrilled, but she felt that she had to go back to work when the infant was five months old. One day while in the classroom, Neva received the message from the day-care center that her lovely little baby had died unexplainably of sudden infant death syndrome. Neva was devastated. She quit teaching because she worried that something might happen to her five-year-old in the day-care center too. She became sterilized so that she would never have another child, because she was afraid it too would die.

Neva had every right to grieve for her baby. Since guilt is a stage of grief, it was natural for her to feel guilty for a time. The fact that she quit teaching because she was so worried about harm befalling the older daughter, however, was a sign that her self-blame had exceeded normal proportions. Neva needed to focus her energies on what she could do to help herself and her remaining child now that the tragedy had occurred.

There is a story about a grieving woman who once brought her dead baby to a Zen master and begged him to find a way to restore it to life. The wise old man said, "Let me have your baby. You go and bring me someone who has never experienced the loss of a loved one, and I will bring him back." Then the mother realized that she was not alone. Everyone who lives long enough loses loved ones. After a loss you cannot go back, but you can move forward.

You may find that even an experience that you view as a tragedy may hold a gift. When Bob was born with a club foot, his parents grieved. When he came of age, however, this disability kept him from having to serve in Vietnam, where he could easily have lost his life. Jane's parents grieved over her burns, but now Jane says, "If it had not been for my burns, I would not have been forced to develop a positive mental attitude. I would not be able to help others see that they too are beautiful inside, despite their scars."

If you are worried about some tragedy that has happened to your child, give yourself permission to grieve for the loss, but don't get stuck in an "If Only" mind-set. If you do feel stuck, here is an exercise that may help you. Sit for a moment and think of something traumatic that happened to you which might have caused your mother to say, "Oh, I can't bear to have this happen to my child." Were you injured physically or emotionally? Did you fail in school? Did a parent die? Did you suffer loss or pain as a child or young adult—or even recently?

Now divide a sheet of paper into three columns labeled "Event," "My Mother's Feelings," and "How I Grew." Write down the traumatic event in the first column, and how your mother must have felt when it happened to you in the second column. Did she feel guilty? Devastated? Sad? Angry?

Now think about ways in which you were forced to grow because of the traumatic event. Just as Jane learned how important it was to feel beautiful inside and how to help others feel that way, you may have grown too. If you were injured, you may have learned to value the small things in life. You may have learned amazing ways to compensate that are an inspiration to others. If you failed in school, you may have learned the importance of studying. Or you may have discovered a previously unthought-of career for which you did not need that kind of education. If your father died, you may have learned how to make your own decisions.

Whatever the pearl is in the oyster of your misfortune, write it down. Then remind yourself that if your children have experienced trauma, they too can find a reward. Set your goal to help your child receive that gift. Use the pink bubble technique to visualize your children overcoming their trauma and even excelling because of it. Release them—and your worry—to the power in the universe which inspires the human spirit to grow through pain. When you are able to give up your anxiety, you will be providing your children with a wonderful gift.

RISKING CHANGE

An article titled "Mother to Mother," in the February 1989 issue of *Parents* magazine, told how to create a mothers' support group. Some mothers organized their own groups simply by asking other women they saw at the supermarket or in the park if they would like to get together for support. Others called on national groups such as La Leche League or The Family Resource Coalition to help. Some focused on the general needs of all parents; others singled out one particular aspect of child-rearing, such as the problems faced by working mothers or parents of twins. We feel that joining such groups is a good way to begin using the Fourth SKILL Tool, letting yourself risk. When you have the support of other mothers, it is easier to change the words, thoughts, and actions that contribute to worry about your children. You may trade ideas about how to communicate with your children, how to discipline constructively, or how to let go of unproductive worrying.

Meanwhile, you can be assertive and use the "So What?" Technique on your own to challenge the many "What Ifs?" that creep in to mothering. Doing this exercise will help you discover the negative thoughts about yourself that are causing you to climb on the worry-go-round rather than to find solutions.

For instance, you might write:

"I'm worried that my daughter persists in sucking her thumb."
"So what?"

"It reflects on me as her mother. I am afraid that people will think I have not given her enough love if she keeps sucking her thumb."

"So what?"

"So I know that I do love her and I don't have to bother with what others think. I am a worthy person even when I make mistakes in child rearing."

How does the "So What?" Technique help the mother who is worried that her son refuses to give up the friends whom she doesn't like? Here's the dialogue:

"I'm worried because my son in running around with the wrong kind of friends."

"So what?"

"So if he has the wrong kind of friends, he might get into vandalism or other misbehavior. That would be terrible for him and I would feel like a failure as a parent."

"So what?"

"So if he does, the police will force us to make restitution, and I will have to punish him. I won't like it, but I can live with it. Plenty of other parents have tried their best and their children have gotten into trouble. It is okay if I'm not perfect. Besides, my son will learn an important lesson about choosing friends, because I will make him earn the money to pay."

By using the "So What?" Technique, you can discover both your feelings and your faulty cognitions. Are you thinking in "My Fault" perfectionism or white-is-black terms when you worry about your children's failures? Are you thinking that you *ought* to be a better parent? Identify which of the Top Ten Cognitive Distortions are the root of your worry about your child. Then write out some affirmations about yourself and your child, such as:

- I am a person of worth no matter what my child is doing. (Admittedly this is a tough one, but it is true!)
- Just as I am responsible for my own actions, my children are responsible for theirs.

- I can choose to be free of worry. This is a way I can help my child.
- Every day my child is getting better and better.

Affirm that you and your child are already the way you want to be. Remember that the less you worry, the more you help your child.

We have to admire Dallasite Wayne Knipe who told us how he used a concern about his children's study habits to pearl worry in a most impressive way. Knipe remembered how his own parents used to tell him, "You're too smart to be making C's in school." As an insurance broker and businessman, however, he realized that the best way to motivate employees was with a business plan that outlined the steps required for achievement. Accordingly, he wrote an illustrated sixteen-page booklet for his children titled *Better Grades Easier*. In it, a dragon, a gorilla, and the Karate Kid promise average students that it is easy to make better grades if the students use their secrets. For instance, they show how to read test questions with the goal of making a better grade, and how to associate amusing pictures with facts in order to memorize information. Knipe's children benefited so much that he published the book. Then the Dallas Independent School District distributed fifteen thousand copies to seventh and eighth graders.

Knipe told us, "Rather than telling my children they ought to be making A's, I wanted to say to them, 'Follow these steps. This is the best I expect from you.'" Knipe risked taking action rather than worrying and nagging his children. He not only helped his own children with their schoolwork and their self-esteem, but helped plenty of others. And he made money, too!

WHEN CAN YOU STOP WORRYING ABOUT CHILDREN?

How many mothers of children in their twenties and thirties do you know who are still debilitated by parental guilt and worry? We know from our experience in helping women that once you are a parent, you will always be concerned for your children, even when they are fifty years old. That is why it is so important to learn to let go of worry when the children are younger. But it is never too late to begin!

We have a dear friend, whom we will call Norma, who waited until she was a grandmother to become assertive in relating to her children. Norma had raised her four children as a single parent. When one son got married and then divorced, Norma worried about her grandchildren. Her son's ex-wife, who was on drugs, neglected the children. Unable to pay the rent, she moved from apartment to apartment every thirty days, taking advantage of deals in which the first month's rent was free. Because the ten-year-old changed schools each month, he had never learned to read. And to Norma's horror, she discovered that he needed several root canals: He had eighteen cavities in his permanent teeth because his diet consisted of junk food. All the grandchildren had lice as well.

For a long time Norma grieved over this situation, but told herself she was helpless to do anything about it. Every day she called her worry partner and played the "ain't it awful" game. Then one day we told Norma that worry doesn't change anything. You either solve a problem or learn how to let go. It turned out that Norma wasn't willing to stand by and watch her grandchildren suffer. She used the Triple A Formula to alter, avoid, and accept her problem. To alter, she sought out professional help. The state's Child Protective Services helped her work out a plan to remove the children from their mother's care for a year, giving the mother a chance to get off drugs and find a job. When Norma communicated assertively with other relatives, she found they were willing to help too. She herself would take care of the ten-year-old. Her son, the father of the children, would take the middle child, and her daughter would take the baby. Each would allow the mother to visit the children whenever she wanted.

To avoid worrying about how everything was going to turn out, Norma used the avoiding techniques and gave up talking with her worry partner. Every time Mr. Negative tormented her with the thought that she couldn't cope, she went to an alpha state and visualized herself and the grandchildren smiling and happy. She used accepting techniques to recognize that solving all of the grandchildren's problems overnight was an unrealistic expectation, but that she would take things one day at a time.

"I used to worry myself sick about my grandchildren, but I didn't do anything to change circumstances," Norma said. "Then I realized that it was up to me to save them. So I got help. And I got everybody involved. Even though it was a lot of work, I feel better now. I can let go of all that terrible worry, because I know that I have done all that is possible."

We were impressed that Norma could stop blaming others and risk constructive actions. She gave of herself, but she did it in such a way that her children and grandchildren could learn to take responsibility for themselves. That's the goal that we hope you will set for yourself, too.

In our opinion, nobody describes the advantages of relating to children without worry better than Kahlil Gibran in *The Prophet:* "You may give them your love, but not your thoughts, for they have their own thoughts. You may house their bodies, but not their souls, for their souls dwell in the house of tomorrow, which you cannot visit, not even in your dreams." By learning to solve the problems only you can solve, letting go of unrealistic expectations, and choosing to think positively, you make it possible for your children to become who they really are. At the same time, you free yourself from the worry-go-round.

CHAPTER 14

◆ ◆ ◆

Using the SKILL Tools to Stop Worrying About Health and Appearance

Jane's friend from Europe, who we'll call Maria, was a natural beauty and a born worrier. After studying to become a skin care specialist, she fretted that her own complexion was not perfect. She spent every cent she had on cosmetics. Then, to her great delight, she was asked to model clothes at a store. A manufacturer used a photo of her legs to promote a hosiery product. Thrilled, she registered with a modeling agency, but the director told her, "You're not quite thin enough to make it to the top." Maria vowed to lose weight, and plenty of it. She began to fast. Food became Public Enemy Number One.

When Maria came to visit Jane, she substituted a glass of water for supper. During the night, however, Maria couldn't sleep. She rummaged around in Jane's kitchen and found a five-pound sack of sweet potatoes. She baked them and ate every one. Then at five in the morning she began to suffer with intestinal cramps. Bloated and miserable, she begged Jane to take her to the hospital.

"At the time I did not understand bulimia, but I did recognize that Maria was sick," Jane said. "She starved herself to lose weight. When hunger overpowered her, she binged. Then she purged herself afterward. The sad part is that Maria started out as a beautiful girl, but she became an empty shell. By worrying so much about her appearance, she endangered her health."

If Maria sounds like an extreme case, she is. But worry over appearance and health is not so unusual. Nearly everyone in our focus groups revealed that they worried about the way they looked and felt. Women reported they were too fat or too thin, or that they had acne or freckles, a bad nose, small or too-large breasts, thin hair or too much of it. They worried about getting old—developing wrinkles, grey hair, and a widow's hump. For some, a real or imaginary flaw in their appearance was their number-one worry.

These women also told us that they feared the "female diseases," such as osteoporosis and breast cancer. They were aware that as women adopt the hard-driving lifestyle traditionally held by men, they now face growing incidences of typically male health problems like heart disease. And AIDS is a growing threat as well.

Unfortunately, the more you worry about illness, the more likely you will bring on bad health. You may not develop bulimia as Maria did, but when you worry excessively about your appearance (or anything else that you perceive as a problem), you raise the level of stress in your internal "rain barrel." When it spills over, your parasympathetic nervous system initiates the fight or flight response to perceived crisis. It spews out adrenaline and other chemicals that make your heart pound, your digestive system shut down, your mouth go dry, and your blood pressure rise. Depending on your genetic makeup and unique vulnerabilities, you may develop panic attacks or stress-related physical problems such as headaches, insomnia, colitis, diarrhea, digestive irregularities, lower back pain, hives, and ulcers.

The new scientific discipline of psychoneuroimmunology has found solid evidence that emotions, mental attitudes, and lack of coping techniques affect the immune system. When you worry, think negatively, or feel unable to solve problems and make decisions, you reduce your body's ability to fight off disease. An article in the April 1989 issue of *Working Woman* magazine quoted Bruce McEwen, Ph.D., professor and head of the laboratory of neuroendocrinology at Rockefeller University in New York City, who said,

"Too much or too little of a particular hormone caused by emotional or physical stress can throw off the immune system, making you more likely to get sick," Your emotions can both trigger the release of hormones and be affected by them.

By using the SKILL Tools to reduce worry, you can combat the stresses that contribute to hives, skin ailments, wrinkles, thin hair, and other problems that detract from your appearance. You may also strengthen your immune system against illness and diseases that women especially fear, like heart problems and uterine or ovarian cancer.

WHY ARE YOU REALLY WORRIED ABOUT YOUR APPEARANCE?

To discover the real reason for your worry about your appearance, use the First SKILL Tool. In your journal, divide a sheet of paper into three columns and label them "What I'm Worried About," "The Real Reason Why," and "Affirmations." If you are worried that you are unattractive, don't write down a general "I'm ugly" or "I'm not as pretty as Mary." Take a good look at yourself in a mirror and then write down as specifically as you can what you consider to be your flaws. Perhaps you think your nose is too big, your complexion is bad, or your hair is a mousy color. Now that you have stated the problem, seek the real reason for your worry.

• *Is your worry psychosocial?* For example, did others tease you about your nose, your complexion, or your hair when you were a child? Is poor self-esteem causing you to feel less attractive than other women even though what you see in the mirror is fairly normal? If you hear yourself saying "I *should*" or "I *ought* to look better", you can feel safe in assessing the problem as a psychosocial one.

Although you can improve your appearance with good grooming and attractive clothes, there may still be some things you don't like about your appearance which you'll just have to accept. Jane says, "I could spend my whole life worrying that my body is scarred and never realize I have a lot of other things going for me. I remind myself that I am athletic. I have agility and a quick mind. I focus on my strengths rather than the one part of me that I consider flawed."

When you write down the reasons for your worry, use the "So What?" technique:

"So what if my nose is big?"
"People will stare."
"So what?
"So I'll feel uncomfortable."
"So what?"
"So it's all right if I feel uncomfortable. Other people don't like some things about themselves either. I'll do what I can with cosmetics and hairstyling to highlight features other than my nose. I'll focus on my nice smile and the fact that I really enjoy other people."

Write down your affirmation: "My nose is okay as it is. I have many strengths. I have a nice smile and I enjoy other people."

• *Is your problem societal?* Do you compare yourself to the glamorous models and actresses in magazine ads, soap operas, and movies? Our society really does reward beauty, and feeling good about your appearance is a boost for your self-confidence. We believe that you should do everything you can to look your best. When you become obsessed with looking like a celebrity or a model, however, you are letting yourself fall into the societal worry trap.

One evening when we were in a theater lobby during intermission, we decided to count the number of women we thought were truly beautiful. Out of the hundreds, we found only two. Yet many were extremely attractive, even though they had features that would not qualify them to be models. They dressed in the right colors and styles to complement their figure and complexion. Their hair styles set off their faces. Their confidence and absence of self-absorbed worry shone through their animated expressions and their erect posture. This little exercise proved what we already knew: Nearly everyone has features about themselves that they don't like, but those who feel good about themselves attract others anyway.

If you are worried that you don't look as beautiful as the models in magazine ads, write down your worry and then use the "So What?" technique:

"So what if I am not beautiful?"
"I feel ugly."
"So what?"
"I don't like feeling ugly."
"So what?"
"So I'll do what I can to improve my looks. I'll give a beautician who specializes in make-overs permission to style my hair differently and select my makeup. I'll ask a friend who dresses attractively to shop with me and make suggestions. Then I will let go of feelings that make me seem unattractive."

Affirm: "I am an attractive person. I like the way I look even though my hair/nose/complexion could use some improvements. I'm taking steps to do just that."

• *Is your worry physiological?* Are you overweight? Is your hair beginning to grey? Do you have wrinkles? As we have pointed out, the real reason why you worry about physical features can be societal or psychosocial. With that in mind, you may opt to accept your physiology, and change the way you think about it, or you may opt to change it, so long as your goal for change is a realistic one. Once Jane complimented a friend on her cute little nose. "Thanks," replied the friend. "I bought it." She went on to tell Jane that she used to have a nose that she thought was awful. Throughout her adolescence she had suffered waves of agony every time anyone looked at her nose. When she became an adult, she underwent plastic surgery. Afterwards, she felt attractive for the first time in her life.

We believe that it is perfectly okay to use modern surgical and beauty techniques to change the shape of your nose, the color of your hair, or anything else that stands in the way of feeling good about yourself. If you really cannot bear some physical feature, then write down that the real reason for your worry is that you can't live with it. Under affirmations, write: "I can take action to change my nose/weight/wrinkles." Use the Third SKILL Tool to image the goals you want to reach. See yourself looking wonderful after plastic surgery by a qualified professional or after a safe and successful weight reduction program. Visualize yourself surrounded by your friends as they tell you that you look great. If you do not want to undergo plastic surgery or take other action steps, we will show you later in this chapter how to use the Fifth SKILL TOOL to let go of your appearance worries.

DISCOVERING ALTERNATIVES TO HEALTH WORRIES

You can use these same questions to discover the real reason for your health worry. Let's say that you are terrified that you are going to develop breast cancer:

• *Is your worry psychosocial?* Do you read a newspaper article about breast cancer and tell yourself, "With my rotten luck, I'll probably get it"? If so, write down that you have been a worrier. Realize that you can choose not to listen to Mr. Negative when he hounds you with information about bad health. Then affirm: "I am now completely free of any worry about breast cancer."

• *Is your worry societal?* Do you have a close friend who has had a mastectomy? Do you have worry partners who trade horror stories about breast cancer? If so, write down these reasons. Affirm: "Just because my friend had a mastectomy is no reason that I will have one. I am perfectly healthy."

• *Is your worry physiological?* Does your family have a history of breast cancer? Do you fit the high-risk profiles as publicized by the American Cancer Society? If so, write down these as reasons for your worry. Affirm that you will discuss your fears with your doctor and follow his or her recommendations about getting mammograms and doing monthly self-examinations.

Since the American Cancer Institute reports that 120,000 cases of breast cancer are discovered each year in the United States, this disease is certainly something to be concerned about. Do everything you can to detect it in an early stage—everything but worry. As the psychoneuroimmunologists report, anxiety may lower your immunity to all disease. You can better protect yourself by accepting the danger as being out of your hands and letting go of the worry. Recognize that millions of women, including Betty Ford and Nancy Reagan, have survived mastectomies and are living happy and fulfilled lives. Anne Gillian, who had a double mastectomy, told her story in an inspiring nationally televised TV movie in 1988. Affirm that you too could adjust.

If you currently have a chronic illness, look for the psychosocial reasons that are a part of your worry. Do you feel that you are sick because you are being punished for something you did in the past? Do you feel that you are a loser? Affirm that you are a worthy person who deserves to feel good. By taking action to reduce such worries, you may improve your health. At the very least, you will free up mental and physical energy to enjoy the benefits you do have, which include life itself.

This theory seems to be borne out by a provocative pilot study presented in a symposium called "Psychoimmunological Factors in Progression of HIV Infection" at the 1989 annual meeting of the American Association for the Advancement of Science. Dr. Karl Goodkin, a psychoneuroimmunologist at the University of Texas Southwestern Medical School at Dallas, who conducted the biopsychosocial research, concluded that positive thinking, social support, and stress reduction may help delay the time it takes for a person with HIV infection to develop AIDS. Of the forty homosexual males in the study, some were infected with HIV, the virus that causes AIDS. Those who had the virus but had not developed AIDS had less stress, more social support, and more effective ways of coping with stress than those who had progressed to AIDS or AIDS-related complex. Dr. Goodkin, who has also been doing research on the impact of stress on the development and course of cervical cancer, said in a statement released by the University of Texas that he has observed that stress can affect the levels of certain hormones in the blood. These hormones can cause changes in immune system cells leading to lowered resistance to certain diseases. While this research is still at the descriptive level and has unknown clinical significance, he was quoted as suggesting that cognitive therapy, relaxation training, and exercise could inhibit disease.

If you have a chronic disease, affirm that you can learn ways to think and act positively about your situation.

USING THE UNCONSCIOUS TO IMPROVE YOUR HEALTH

In his fascinating book, _Quantum Healing_, author Deepak Chopra, M.D., details evidence for the theories that Indian yogis have believed for centuries: The body has its own "mind." Each cell performs its amazingly intricate purpose in accordance with this intelligence. When one organ is sick, all the other organs know it and react. By the same token, when you relax, visualize yourself as feeling well, and change your thought processes, the whole body hears this message and responds. Dr. Chopra tells the startling story of a woman who thought she had gallstones. The surgeon found instead that she had inoperable cancer. Since her family requested that she not be informed, the surgeon simply told her that she did not have gallstones after all. "Great," said the patient, who assumed that she would be well and able to do everything she wanted. Amazingly enough, she did get well, and Dr. Chopra believes that it was because her body received the message, "I am well," and went about healing itself.

Bob also discovered the healing power of the mind when he was recovering from agoraphobia. When he learned to relax and program his unconscious to be free of the terrible symptoms of panic attacks, he was able to leave his home and practice desensitizing himself to his fear. At the same time, he got over the very physical problem of chronic colitis, which had plagued him for years.

If you are already sick or if you worry about becoming sick, use the Third SKILL Tool. Go to the alpha state (as described in chapter 8) at least three times a day and program your unconscious using visualizations and affirmations that you have created beforehand. For instance, if you want to be free of headaches, write this goal on a sheet of paper: "I am completely free of headaches." Then construct and write down a three-stage visualization:

1. See yourself experiencing the pain of a headache. What colors, shapes, and sounds would describe this? Use all your senses to create a powerful image. You might imagine yourself with a fiery red face with black light streaming from your head.

2. Now see yourself drawing a big black X over this vision of yourself.

3. See your face with its normal healthy color and your head surrounded by a white light that shimmers into a rainbow of beautiful colors.

After constructing your three steps, go to the alpha state and create the first visualization. Next, draw the X on it. Then erase this picture of yourself completely. Immediately replace it with the third visualization. Spend a few moments seeing yourself this way while you affirm that you are free of headaches.

Both of us have used our unconscious in this way to stop a headache. You can use the unconscious to combat many illnesses. Books like Bob's *Anxiety and Panic Attacks* and *Beyond Fear*, Carl Simonton's *Getting Well Again*, Bernie Siegel's *Love, Medicine & Miracles*, and Chopra's *Quantum Healing* will show you how to use visualizations for everything from weight loss and panic attacks to diabetes, heart problems, and cancer.

Please keep in mind that *we are not saying that you should not go to your doctor if you are sick*. We believe in using every medical tool available. That is truly taking action rather than worrying. We also urge you to recognize that you have your own internal healing processes to help you recover. To encourage patients who want to tap into this power, Bernie Siegel has started a therapy group called Exceptional Cancer Patients for the 15 percent to 20 percent of his patients who "refuse to play the victim," according to a story in the May 14, 1989, issue of the *Dallas Morning News*. These patients keep control of their own bodies and become responsible participants in their health care to become survivors, Siegel said.

You don't have to wait until you get sick to use these techniques. If you worry about getting sick, go to the alpha state and program your unconscious with affirmations and visualizations of continuing good health.

RISKING ACTION TO
IMPROVE YOUR HEALTH

"Success is turning knowledge into positive action." That is the credo of our friend, Dorothy Leeds, author of *Smart Questions: A New Strategy for Successful Managers*. When she was diagnosed as having breast cancer in 1982, she found that positive action also brought rewards in her health.

"The night the doctor told me I would have to have a mastectomy, I had a terrible fear that I would die within three months. But I didn't want a mastectomy either, so I checked out of the hospital and spent three weeks researching the lumpectomy, which was then a controversial method of treatment. I contacted seven other doctors for their opinions, and then made my decision to have a lumpectomy," she told us. "I was lucky in that I had a very small tumor which made lumpectomy possible. I'm glad that I took responsibility for my own treatment. Because I was putting my energy into action rather than worry, I was able to act in a way that saved me from a mastectomy."

As Dorothy says when she leads training seminars for major corporations, "All of us know a tremendous amount, but knowing and doing are two different things. We have to take action to make things happen, but most people don't take action because they worry about what will happen if they do."

Once you have used the unconscious to overcome the worry and fear associated with taking action, then use the Fourth SKILL Tool: Risk participating in healthy routines that will not only help you get well or stay well but will also reduce your worry, because they help you feel more in control of your well-being. Here are some tips:

• *Adopt better eating habits.* Rather than worry about whether you're increasing your cholesterol, developing hypoglycemia, or adding unwanted pounds because of your eating habits, risk changing your diet. Study your nutritional needs and change your eating habits so that you can stay fit. When you feel better, anxiety diminishes.

One morning Jane didn't have time to eat breakfast before going to work. "About ten in the morning I felt a little tired, so I bought two cups of black coffee, laced them with sugar, and ate a candy bar to go with them. That afternoon I suddenly felt sick. I was so fatigued that I couldn't function. I had to leave the office. I almost panicked, wondering what terrible illness I had. Then I thought about the caffeine and sugar. I'd always known they weren't good for me, but now it seemed that my body was sending me a signal to stop eating them right that minute. So I did. I gave up coffee and sugar 'cold turkey.' Two weeks later I felt so much better that I wondered why I hadn't done it long ago," Jane said.

Dr. John C. LaRosa of George Washington University Medical Center, the past chairman of the American Heart Association's nutrition committee, says that some people skip breakfast to save calories, but breakfast is extremely important. "You haven't eaten for eight or ten hours and you need the energy that breakfast provides," he says in the AHA's "HeartStyle" newsletter. He advocates low-cholesterol, high-fiber breakfasts like cold cereal with fruit juice.

When Bob discovered he needed to lose twenty-seven pounds after he recovered from agoraphobia, he risked going on a twelve-hundred-calorie-a-day diet. He set up a sensible eating plan that included foods from the four necessary food groups—milk, meat, vegetables and fruits, and bread and cereal. Losing weight made him feel better physically. He knew that he looked better, too, so he did not have to worry about his appearance.

• *Follow a daily exercise schedule.* Once Bob had begun to lose weight, he discovered that exercise was essential if he wanted to keep the pounds off. He took up jogging as a means of weight control. By participating in this activity, he discovered an added benefit: the runner's "high" from endorphins that cancels out a lot of worries.

Dr. Kenneth Cooper, of the Aerobics Center in Dallas, explains that most people today don't have a physical outlet for stress as did primitive humans, who needed the body's hormonal response to help them fight or flee from danger. "As a result, when you're keyed up from a high level of adrenal hormones, your body is chemically out of balance. . . . Exercise increases metabolism, which helps eliminate the effect of the accumulated adrenal secretions. Walking actually acts as nature's waste removal process, helping the body return to a more relaxed state," he said in the March 1989 issue of "Fit Tips," a newsletter published by the Aerobics Center of Dallas.

• *Stop smoking.* In November 1987, more than 19.5 million smokers, (more than 39 percent of the nation's 50 million smokers) tried to quit for twenty-four hours during the Great American Smokeout. We can't emphasize enough how important it is to quit. While breast cancer used to be the leading cause of death among women, today it is lung cancer. If you smoke, you are bound to worry about it, so take action. Use our tools to help you. Call the American Cancer Society for information on professional help in your area.

• *Get enough sleep.* You may be too tired to feel or look your best. According to a press release from the University of Texas Southwestern Medical Center at Dallas, Dr. Howard Roffwarg, an internationally known sleep researcher, reports that somewhere between 10 and 20 percent of chronic insomniacs are caught up in a vicious circle. They worry so much about sleeping that they can't go to sleep. They may even learn to associate their own bed with not being able to sleep. That is why one of Roffwarg's patients, a mountain climber, had the best night's sleep he had had in a long time when he was forced to spend a stormy night lashed to a small ledge on a mountain. He slept well because he was not expecting to sleep at all. If you cannot overcome your insomnia by using visualizations and affirmations or by exercise and nutrition, you may want to seek professional help.

• *Develop a sense of humor.* At a seminar we attended, Arnold Fox, author of the *Beverly Hills Medical Diet*, asked everyone to laugh for 15 seconds. We didn't have anything funny to laugh about, but he encouraged us to break out in tremendous hee-haws. We thought he was crazy but we did it, and afterward we felt relaxed. Everyone in the room seemed to lighten up—even though they were *faking* humor. Fox explained that laughing releases endorphins which give you a natural high. Laughter also may help to heal. In his inspiring book, *Anatomy of an Illness*, Norman Cousins credited laughter, vitamin C, and his will to live as the cure for his ankylosing spondylitis, a crippling disease that most doctors consider irreversible. Laughter is a wonderful way to reduce pain, promote healing, and stop worrying.

USING THE UNCONSCIOUS TO IMPROVE YOUR APPEARANCE

Our friend and professional speaker, Toni Blake, participated in a weight reduction program that included behavior modification. Only then did she realize that she had been using food to "pad up" and protect herself against dealing with issues. Toni had never believed that she was beautiful. Her misperception started in childhood when her family teased her about being the only redhead. While her family loved her dearly, Toni felt hurt. She even imagined that she must have been adopted. After the healing of her emotions and a year in the program, Toni lost an amazing 60 pounds. Now she dreams of starting her speeches with an impressive before-and-after visual aid. After her introduction she would walk out, slim and svelte, from behind a life-size photo of herself when she was overweight.

"Before I changed my weight, I changed my mind. I used different words to think about myself, and the result was positive action," Toni said. By using the unconscious mind you can change your perception of yourself. You may not be able to improve the structure of your cheekbones, but you can increase your self-esteem enough to make the most of what you already have. You can lose weight, start doing fitness routines, and develop hobbies that will make you feel energized and excited about life.

Set your goal: "I will lose _____ (number of pounds). Create visualizations of yourself as a slender woman. See yourself eating nutritious low-calorie meals while you affirm that you crave fresh vegetables and that your favorite drink is water. See yourself in an aerobics class with a smile on your face and affirm that you enjoy the activity. Then go to an alpha state at least three times a day and use these visualizations in your programming.

LETTING GO OF APPEARANCE PROBLEMS

When Jane makes speeches about self-improvement, she often says, "Some of us are genetic celebrities—and some of us look like the dickens." It is healthy to improve yourself, but it is also self-affirming to recognize that you don't have to look model-perfect. It is even better when you can laugh about yourself. If you have decided to accept some feature about yourself that you don't like, use the Fifth SKILL Tool to make it easier. Ask yourself if your problem is beyond your control. Are you six-feet-two when you would prefer to be a petite five feet tall? Are you proportioned in such a way that no matter how many pounds you lose, your hips will be bigger than you'd like them to be?

We have to admire how our friend Jan Kirkman accepted and made the most of having had alopecia universalis, a complete, irreversible loss of hair over her entire body. Not only is she completely bald, but she even lacks eyebrows and eyelashes. With wigs and makeup she successfully hid this condition for thirty-three years. When she decided to go public with her secret, she chose a dramatic way to do it. She gave a humorous speech describing her experiences. Her role models, she said, were Mr. Clean, Telly Savalas, and Yul Brynner. She was glad that she could leave her hair at the cleaners (the wig stylists) rather than having to sit under a hot dryer. Then she told of the tremendous support of her husband, Bill, who told her: "I don't love you for what's on top of your head but what's inside of you."

You may not be willing to call attention as this friend did to something about your body that you don't like, but you can get off the worry-go-round about it. Accept the flaws and put limits on the amount of time you will worry about your appearance. Go to an alpha state and see others appreciating you just as you are. Whenever you are inclined to worry, distract yourself with interesting activities and hobbies. Then make the most of the assets that you do have. If you are a large woman, for example, go to the shops that specialize in your sizes and choose the most attractive clothes that you can find.

At a time when Jane was feeling insecure about her self-worth, she attended a self-improvement seminar. Jane couldn't feel good about herself unless she wore jeans that were two sizes too small, a skimpy tank top, and enough eye makeup to paint a mural. The friend who went with her, whom we'll call Pam, expressed her insecurity in a different way. She hid herself in shapeless tweeds and wore no makeup at all.

"One of the exercises was to come to the next day's meeting dressed as the exact opposite of our perception of ourselves" Jane recalls. "That meant that I had to put on loose-fitting clothes, leave my hair uncurled and scrub my face clean of makeup. Pam dressed the way I usually did. When I arrived the next day in my droopy clothes and naked face, I felt like hiding in a corner. I felt as if my eyes didn't even exist! Even worse, Pam was getting a lot of attention because she looked wonderful. After awhile, however, several people told me, 'Jane, you look so much better. You look softer, more real.' Then I realized that the real Jane was okay, even without makeup and sexy clothes."

We believe that the most attractive thing about a woman is the way she feels about herself. When you can accept yourself as you are and not feel that you have to depend on makeup, jewelry, and flashy clothes, you will be attractive from the inside out—and others will notice this positive change.

LETTING GO OF HEALTH PROBLEMS

In *Love, Medicine & Miracles*, Bernie Siegel, M.D., says that living means being 100 percent alive and vital. We agree. If you worry all the time about health problems, it is like being dead, even if you are perfectly healthy. You are not letting yourself enjoy the life that you're living this very moment!

W Mitchell, a professional speaker and friend, survived a motorcycle accident but was so badly burned that his face was disfigured. He lost most of his fingers too. In his speeches, he tells how one day the plastic surgeon asked to see his driver's license. The doctor inspected the photo on the license and then said, "Oh, so that's what you used to look like? Well, we can do better than that." After years of surgery, Mitchell's appearance did improve. Then he was in a plane crash and became a paraplegic. How did Mitchell deal with this second tragedy?

"It's not what happens in your life, but what you do with what happens," he tells his audiences. How easy it would be for Mitchell to give up, turn his face to the wall and exist as if he were already dead. Instead he has a speaking career and is a successful businessman as well. He can be proud of motivating others to live their lives a better way. (By the way, he has a beautiful wife too.)

If you have a chronic disease, it's important to learn to live in the present moment. Draw an X over the malicious pictures of disability or catastrophe in your mind and immediately replace them with visualizations of yourself looking well and happy and enjoying your favorite moments in life. Make a list of all the good things in your life. Determine how you can reach out to others so you can enjoy the good feelings you will have when you help someone else.

BE KIND TO YOURSELF

Many worries related to health and appearance are "should" and "ought" related. "I *should* look and feel better than this" or "I *ought* to be exercising and eating right," you tell yourself. If you are lecturing yourself in this way, you may be thinking in perfectionistic terms. You have two options for being kind to yourself: Either set your goal to improve your appearance and health, or stop the fussing and let your emotional self feel better! Use the SKILL Tools to get off the worry-go-round. Pearl worry instead and receive the wonderful gift of looking and feeling better.

CHAPTER 15

◆ ◆ ◆

Banishing Worries That Lead to Irrational Fears

"When I got an invitation to a party which my ex-boyfriend was going to attend, I was worried," Phyllis told her focus group. "I tried to picture myself saying something cool and calm to Peter, but my imagination kept running away with me. First I would see him putting me down, then I would see myself retaliating, and before I could stop it we were throwing hors d'oeuvres at each other. Whenever I thought about the party, my heart would start pounding and my hands would get sweaty. It was going to be a catastrophe!"

Fortunately Phyllis took stock and realized that she was imagining exactly what she did *not* want to happen rather than taking control and using her unconscious to create solutions. She made the choice to sit down and write out some pleasant, innocuous comments she could make to Peter at the party. Then she relaxed and visualized herself at the party feeling calm, peaceful, and happy. If, despite her intentions, her imagination ran away with her and showed her visions of Peter being abusive, she drew a big X over the picture in her mind and immediately replaced it with an image of herself smiling and making the comments she had written down. She affirmed that she felt perfectly calm whenever she saw Peter. By programming herself in this way before the party, Phyllis amazed everyone with her composure when she actually faced Peter.

It is entirely normal to worry over a stressful event like running into an ex-boyfriend at a party, but as Phyllis discovered, the SKILL Tools can help tame the anxiety. Let's see what might have happened if Phyllis had not taken control of the catastrophic scenarios: Feeling nervous and angry even before arriving, Phyllis would be unable to contain her anger if Peter needled her. She would make a scene. Humiliated, she might go home and play the "What will other people think?" game. Tired and distracted by constantly replaying the embarrassing scene in her head, she might make a serious mistake at work. That would be the final blow! Maybe she would start having trouble talking to men at parties, recalling her bad episode with Peter and the pain of that broken relationship. In time, she might become so ill at ease that she would begin to avoid going to parties.

If Phyllis should continue with this kind of anxiety long enough, she might spiral into what the American Psychological Association's *Diagnostic and Statistical Manual of Mental Disorders* describes as Generalized Anxiety Disorder (GAD)—persistent anxiety of at least six months. This condition is more serious than transient anxiety, and many Americans suffer from it. A recent Gallup Poll says that 30 percent to 40 percent of the general population shows signs of marked anxiety, with more women reporting symptoms than men. The American Psychological Association now considers anxiety disorders the most prevalent psychiatric complaint.

With GAD, Phyllis also runs the risk of developing phobias or panic attacks. A phobia is an irrational fear of an object or activity which does not cause fear in most people. About 28 million Americans have phobias. They are the most common anxiety disorder for women, according to a survey conducted in five representative cities by the National Institutes of Mental Health.

Here's how Phyllis might develop a phobia: She would keep dwelling on the embarrassment of her public fight with Peter. She would tell herself that she made a fool of herself and vividly imagine the same scenario happening again. Finally she would tell herself, "I'm so jittery and nervous that I can't go to parties. I just don't do well at parties. I'm too afraid."

Like Bob, Phyllis might one day have a panic attack. Her body would generate the fight or flight response for no apparent reason and the symptoms would feel terrifying. If she tried to avoid the places where panic attacks kept happening, she might ultimately develop agoraphobia, the most serious phobia of all, and might decide that her only "safe place" was her home. If so, she would be housebound with fear.

If you develop GAD, phobias, or panic attacks, are you crazy? Certainly not. Many professionals who treat these disorders believe that some people are born with a predisposition for anxiety. If you have chemical or hormonal imbalances, mitral valve prolapse (a bulging of a cardiac valve which may cause dizziness, palpitations, shortness of breath, fatigue, or panic) hypoglycemia, hyperthyroidism, anemia, or hypersensitivity to caffeine, you may be subject to anxiety. If so, are you fated to have phobias and panic attacks? Not at all. You may develop these problems if you let worry and anxiety take control of you. You have the choice to use your mind, as Phyllis and Bob did, to block catastrophic thinking.

In *Anxiety and Panic Attacks*, Bob describes five basic principles that he used to recover from GAD, phobias, and panic attacks. You too can learn to handle stress in a positive way so that you don't develop irrational fears, even if you have a predisposition for them.

HOW WORRY DEVELOPS INTO IRRATIONAL FEARS

In preceding chapters, we described the process whereby worry, negative thoughts, and gloomy daydreams can increase the level of stress in your interior rain barrel until it spills over. Within seconds, your body releases a surge of adrenaline to call in the fight or flight response and you may have a panic attack.

If this happens while you are reading the *Wall Street Journal* (as Bob was), while you are driving a car, making a speech, or having lunch with a friend, you may not understand what is happening. You will likely feel very much afraid, because the symptoms can be so sudden and feel like a heart attack or just plain inexplicable. Not realizing that a fight or flight response is a perfectly normal body reaction, you may avoid any activity or place which you believe caused those terrible feelings.

Even if you never have panic attacks, the arousal symptoms of GAD may be uncomfortable enough to make you want to avoid certain places or activities. Your hands and legs may shake when you get on an airplane, your voice may choke up when you start to make a speech, or you may feel nauseated when you cross a bridge. When you start avoiding these things which other people don't find unduly frightening, you have a phobia. Here is a list of the many kinds of phobias people have:

- *Simple phobias* involve anxiety over a situation like riding elevators, flying, or crossing bridges.
- *Animal phobias* are a fear of insects, snakes, dogs or other creatures.
- *Social phobias* concern fears of making a fool of yourself in front of others. You might fear making speeches, eating alone in a restaurant, going to a party, or making a cold sales call.
- *Agoraphobia* is the fear of fear, which causes you to avoid places where panic attacks have spontaneously occurred. Since the attacks continue, every place eventually becomes off-limits except your "safe place," which is usually your home.

If you are phobic, remember that you do not really fear airplanes, elevators, snakes, or places outside of your home. You fear feeling the arousal symptoms, or the fight or flight response. Because the feelings of fear are caused by a rush of adrenaline, the discomfort will go away within a few minutes if you take control.

RECOVERING FROM A PHOBIA

Professionals disagree about the best approach to recovering from phobias. Many prescribe drugs that block the fear sensations even though they have side effects and may be addictive with long-term use. Some analytical psychiatrists believe that you must remain in therapy for months or even years to explore the unconscious reasons for your phobia. Nearly all agree, however, that a good tool to use is desensitization. This means exposing yourself in many small steps to the object or activity you avoid while at the same time changing your thoughts about what is happening. (This may be easier to do if a friend who has learned some simple coaching techniques goes with you.) If the fear symptoms arise, you allow them to come while you stay with the situation for as long as you can. The key to making desensitization work is increasing your exposure to the feared object or activity very gradually.

Bob, for instance, recovered from agoraphobia by taking a big risk: He started leaving his house; at first going only to the front yard, then down the block, and finally to a neighborhood shopping center. At first he didn't try to enter the supermarket. He just sat in his car looking at it and then drove home. The next step was to enter the store and immediately walk out; then to enter, wheel a grocery cart down one aisle, and leave; and finally to enter, choose an item, and pay for it. Whenever he felt his heart start pounding and his mouth going dry, he reminded himself that the fight or flight response was a perfectly normal body function. He stayed quietly where he was rather than run away.

Paula used desensitization to overcome her driving phobia. Paula liked to go places if someone else drove, but if she had to drive the car, she felt panicky. She sometimes feared that she might aim her car directly at a pedestrian. Paula's therapist helped her desensitize by first sitting with her in the car while they watched traffic pass by. He encouraged her to bring photos of her children and a long-beloved teddy bear so that the car would have a homey feel. Then Paula started driving with her therapist on traffic-free roads. Next she progressed to out-of-the-way, low-traffic highways and then to busy streets. Eventually Paula was able to drive alone.

If you depend solely on medication to control your fear thoughts, you run the risk of relapsing when you stop taking pills. If you desensitize yourself, the results can be permanent without chemical dependency. Our SKILL Tools can make it easier for you to overcome your worries by giving you the emotional strength to try desensitization, and the power of the unconscious will calm you.

SEEKING THE REASON FOR YOUR IRRATIONAL FEAR

The First SKILL Tool will help you identify the actions you need to take to work successfully on desensitization. Ask yourself:

• *Does my phobia have a psychosocial basis?* When I'm eating alone in a restaurant, do I feel that everyone is looking at me? When I present a report at work, am I afraid that I'll make a fool of myself? Do I fear going to a large party where I might clam up and have nothing to say? Do I walk up six flights of stairs instead of riding the elevator and refuse to tell my husband because I'm afraid he will think I'm crazy?

If you answered yes to these questions, you may have been influenced by a traumatic experience which has undermined your self-esteem. Phoebe, for instance, knew why she had claustrophobia, a fear of closed-in places. When she was four years old, she climbed into a big box in which a piano had been delivered. Somehow the lid got stuck, and she couldn't get out. The box was in the alley where no one could hear her cries, so she was trapped for two miserable hours. Now she "can't breathe right" if she must shut the door to her small office. She won't ride elevators. Driving home, she goes miles out of her way rather than pass through a tunnel. Phoebe puts herself down because of her phobia. "No one else is afraid to go in an elevator. I must be crazy," she tells herself. Phoebe needs to desensitize herself to her fear of closed in places and needs to challenge her worry thoughts about herself.

If you, like Phoebe, have had a traumatic childhood experience, write it down. Then affirm, "I can recover from this phobia through desensitizing myself and changing my perceptions of myself."

• *Is your phobia instinctive?* Human beings are born with the fear of falling and the fear of loud noises. For some, these instinctive fears escalate into phobias of heights and of noisy, busy places. Are you afraid to look out of the window of a high-rise building? Do you fear crossing a bridge, climbing a ladder, or driving along a hillside? Are you too nervous to go to a noisy shopping mall or a concert? If you answered yes, your instinctive fear has evolved into a full-fledged phobia. You may not be able to remember any traumatic incident that initiated your phobia; you just know that your hands sweat, your heart pounds, and your mouth goes dry when you do those things. You keep thinking, "What if the ladder falls?", or "What if we drive off a cliff?", or "What if I pass out because of all these people and this noise in the mall?" If your phobia began with an instinctive fear, write it down in your journal. Then affirm, "I can get over this phobia by desensitizing myself and choosing to think positively rather than negatively."

• *Is your phobia based on societal issues?* Do you have so much to think about between your career and your personal life that you feel nervous and on edge all the time? Are you afraid that you just can't compete with the men in your firm for promotions? Do you worry that you might overdress one day and appear too drab the next? Today women face more choices in careers and relationships than their mothers ever did. To be true to themselves, they must take risks. The result is often constant high-level anxiety.

Priscilla first noticed that she was becoming anxious after the birth of her baby. She could not find a quality day-care center and every morning she felt her stomach clutch when she left her son with an attendant who didn't seem to care about him. She also worried that she didn't spend enough quality time with her husband anymore, either. She told herself that the attractive women in his office spent more time with him than she did. They worked side by side and even went to lunch with him. Would he end up having an affair? She felt more and more fatigued, jittery, and distracted at work. Then her grandmother died, and she realized for the first time that she, herself, was not immortal. Priscilla had her first panic attack one morning when she walked into her office, but it wasn't the last. She had so many that she resigned from her job. Eventually Priscilla was housebound with agoraphobia.

Not everyone who is influenced by societal issues develops agoraphobia. You may simply have GAD symptoms. You may feel nervous or have some kind of stress-induced illness, and work may seem doubly hard.

If you have GAD symptoms, write in your journal, "I can learn problem-solving and decision-making skills that will enable me to manage my stress. I do not have to feel anxious." If you already have agoraphobia, affirm, "I know that I can recover because Bob and many others have recovered by using his methods."

• *Is the basis for your phobia physiological?* Do you need a couple of strong cups of coffee to get your creative juices flowing every morning, but find yourself feeling down an hour or so later? Do you have chemical or hormonal imbalances, mitral valve prolapse, hypoglycemia, hyperthyroidism, anemia, or hypersensitivity to caffeine? Have you always been very sensitive to anxiety stimuli? If so, you may have a physical predisposition to anxiety and phobias. That doesn't necessarily mean you will have a problem, however, unless you also tell yourself that you are anxious and scared.

Negative thinking, low self-esteem, and worry led Bob from anxiety straight to panic attacks and agoraphobia. Although others congratulated him on having started his own executive search firm, he perceived himself as not being as successful as he should be. "If people knew the real me, they wouldn't like me," was his feeling. Bob was living in a worried, anxious state without even knowing it. To recover from agoraphobia, he not only needed to desensitize; he had to overcome negative thinking, improve his self-esteem, and learn to block worry.

If you know that you have a physical predisposition to anxiety, in your journal write, "I can change my diet and exercise routine to alleviate physical problems. Even though I have a predisposition to phobias, I am perfectly capable of following Bob's plan for recovery."

ALTERING YOUR PHOBIC BEHAVIOR

Use the Second SKILL Tool's "Triple A" Formula for overcoming the worry that escalates into panic. Here are some ideas:

1. *Alter* the conditions that cause worry.
   • *Challenge catastrophic "What If?" thinking by using the "So, What?" Technique.* Wear a rubber band around your wrist and every time you hear yourself asking "What If?" questions, immediately counter with "So what?" and snap the rubber band. You can train yourself to stop thinking of disastrous consequences and start thinking of solutions.

Because Rachel had a fear of public speaking, she couldn't stand up at business meetings and give reports without getting so nervous that she made a bad impression. "I was always asking myself, 'What if someone asks a question and I can't think what to say?' or 'What if my voice shakes so badly everyone will know I am afraid?' " she told us. Here's how she used the "So What?" technique:

"What if I can't think of anything to say?"

"So what?"

"So everyone will think I'm stupid."

"So what?"

"So I won't get promoted."

"So what?"

"So I'd better do something about it. I'll join Toastmasters like Bob did and get over my phobia."

• *Replace your worry partners with a support person.* Who needs friends who trade horror stories about "the time I got stuck in the elevator?" Instead, you need someone who will help you gradually expose yourself to riding in an elevator by going with you and telling you that you're doing fine. If you have worry partners who persist in scaring you, tell them, "I'm not willing to listen to this."

2. *Avoid* your worries.

• *Distract yourself from your fears.* Therapists often ask agoraphobics to measure the intensity of their fear on a scale of one to ten. Sweaty hands might be a two, while a full-blown panic attack would be a ten. If a client starts having fear symptoms, the therapist will ask her to describe what she is feeling. "It feels like a five. My heart is beating pretty hard," the client might say. Then the therapist might ask her to describe the dress she is wearing, or the color of the chair in which she is sitting, or the decor of the room. The therapist knows that no one can think of two different things at the same time, so she distracts her client from the fear. You can do the same thing without a therapist. If you are thinking of how to describe your fear, or the room, or the dress, you can't be thinking, "I'm making a fool of myself!" If you can distract yourself long enough from your fear, the adrenaline rush will wear off and you will feel calm again.

If you are afraid to fly, distract yourself from your fear by talking to your seat partner, counting by threes or describing to yourself the costume worn by the flight attendant.

- *Say no to Mr. Negative.* If you are constantly worried about your work performance and competition with men, write out some affirmations about yourself, such as: "I am perfectly competent to do my work," or "Every day my work is getting better and better," or "Because I am a woman I have special gifts for this job." Then go to an office supply house and buy some blue dot stickers. Place stickers in strategic places, such as on your telephone, your Daytimer, your watch, or your word processor. Every time your eye falls on a blue dot, ask yourself what you are thinking. If you are thinking something negative about yourself (and you may be surprised at how often you are doing this), immediately cancel that thought and say one of your affirmations.

3. *Accept* your fears.
- *Use attitudinal healing.* Love yourself, even when you aren't perfect. If you have catastrophic thoughts of embarrassing things that could happen to you if you stand up before an audience, consider what really happened to Jane. Once when she was conducting a business seminar before an audience that was mostly male, the cord to her microphone twisted around her leg, causing her to fall off the stage. Even worse, the cord pulled her skirt up so high that if she tried to stand up, her underwear would be exposed.

"For a moment I just lay there. I knew that I wasn't hurt, but I didn't know what to do. Finally a woman came out of the audience and helped me stand while she pulled down my skirt. I got back on the stage and told the audience, 'Well, I gave you more than you paid for!' Everyone laughed and I was able to continue.

"A few weeks later, the program director for that company told me he had seen a video of my speech—and the fall. I thought he was going to tell me that I had made a spectacle of myself and that he never wanted me to conduct another seminar. Instead he laughed with me about my predicament and gave me a contract for another seminar!" Jane said.

Even if the worst possible thing happens when you make a speech, remember that *you will survive*. Consider the audience your friend. Remind yourself that the nervous, shaky fear symptoms are the same feelings you get when you are excited. Remember how excited you are about what you're going to share with the audience. Use those feelings to put energy into your speech.

These alternatives are only a few that you can use to stave off the symptoms of irrational fear. Consult Bob's *Beyond Fear* for other strategies to use.

STOPPING IRRATIONAL FEARS WITH THE IMAGINATION

Our Third SKILL Tool can help you relax your body and reprogram your unconscious to direct your body to remain calm. When Bob was recovering from agoraphobia, he used to go to an alpha state six times a day. He not only released nervous tension but he also imaged himself as being perfectly calm while he was exposing himself to trips away from home. He was then able to go to the supermarket because his unconscious was telling him, "You've already been here and you felt perfectly calm."

Becca knew that she was in a dead-end job, but she feared that she would be too nervous to make a good impression at a job interview. She learned how to program her unconscious by using what we call Emotional Transfusion. She went to an alpha state several times a day and visualized herself in a place where she felt calm and secure. For her, this place was a feather bed at her grandmother's house. She spent several minutes just enjoying the cozy feelings she had experienced there. Then she visualized herself interviewing for a job. Whenever her imagination tried to run away with her and she saw herself stammering and nervous, she drew an X over the scene. She went back to the feather bed, felt the calm feelings, and *transfused* these feelings to the scene of herself in an interviewer's office. She affirmed that she was feeling perfectly calm and in control, that she was answering questions with confidence, and that the interviewer liked her. Emotional Transfusion turned interviewing into an exciting game for Becca. Before long, she had a better job.

If you would like to use Emotional Transfusion, first write out an experience that made you feel calm, happy, and successful. Bob likes to remember the elation of almost hitting a hole in one during a golf game at Pebble Beach, for instance. Some people remember the peace of floating on a raft in a beautiful lake, listening to the sound of birds, or feeling the sun on their face. Others remember the ecstasy of listening to their favorite symphony. When in an alpha state, practice seeing yourself there. Enjoy the good feelings. Then transfer them into a visualization of a situation that you fear.

THINKING YOUR WAY OUT OF AN IRRATIONAL FEAR

Use the Fourth SKILL Tool to let yourself risk uncovering the feelings and thoughts about yourself that may cause you to have irrational fears. The worry about what other people will think of you is the basis for many social phobias. When you get off the worry-go-round by affirming your self-worth, you overcome these phobias, and you can go to parties, speak up at business meetings, eat alone in a restaurant, or go after a new account.

Divide a sheet of paper into two columns labeled "My Distorted Thoughts" and "The Truth." Now use the Inner Critic's Top Ten List of Cognitive Distortions from chapter 9 to discover which ones are fueling your worry. Write down this thought: "Whenever I tell myself that I can't eat at a restaurant alone because everyone else has someone to sit with, my inner critic is telling me I'm being rejected." In the second column, write the truth: "I don't know any of these people in the restaurant, so I can scarcely be rejected. It is perfectly all right for me to eat alone. I feel good about myself."

Because the basis of most social phobias is the irrational fear that you will somehow make a fool of yourself in the presence of others (which in turn stems from low self-esteem), refuse to answer Mr. Negative. Use the blue dot technique described earlier to discover when you are telling yourself you look foolish. You also can wear a rubber band on your wrist, and snap it whenever you have these distorted cognitions. Immediately replace your self-criticism with an affirmation about yourself.

While many experts believe that shyness is an inherited trait, they also believe that distorted cognitions play a part. Every-one in the office told Renee that she was shy. When others spoke to her in the hall, she ducked her head and pretended not to see them. After work she hurried home and settled down with a book. Renee wanted to have friends, dates, and fun, but she had an irrational fear of other people. She did not even feel up to participating in the conversations that went on around the office coffee pot.

When Renee checked the Top Ten Cognitive Distortions, she discovered that she was thinking like a perfectionist. "Whenever I try to converse with others, I make stupid remarks that are either laughed at or ignored. If I can't speak as well as anyone else, it is better not to try at all." Renee blasted her destructive inner critic by writing out and affirming the truth: "I don't have to worry about making the perfect comment. Because I am a worthy person, whatever I say has value." Then she began to desensitize herself to her fear of speaking to others. At first she practiced saying hello to people at the coffee station. Then she planned ahead what else she might say that would be of interest. Using a tape recorder, she practiced talking about the latest book she had read. When she finally did start talking, people responded to her so warmly that she was encouraged to open up even more. Renee was on the pathway to overcoming her excessive shyness.

Be assertive with yourself! Change what you are telling yourself about your irrational fear. Since feelings follow thoughts, you can change your feelings of fear by replacing distorted thinking with affirmations.

LETTING GO

To use our Fifth SKILL Tool, let go of the temptation to say that you can't do anything about your irrational fear. As Bob has so well demonstrated, you *do* have control. The insidious thing about phobias is that they have a payoff. If you "can't" make a speech or drive your car, someone has to do it for you. If you are afraid of flying, you can't be expected to do the things for your company that would help you progress on your job, and you can remain at a low-level, unstressful position. You don't have to develop the gifts that you were born with.

Perhaps you are telling yourself that your phobia doesn't really interfere with your life so you shouldn't waste time trying to get over it. It may be true that minor phobias such as an irrational fear of a snake might never limit your enjoyment of life. But remember that it is all too easy to rationalize. You may tell yourself that it isn't causing you a bit of trouble to spend three days riding a train when you could fly across the nation in a few hours, or that it's good exercise to climb stairs so who needs elevators? That's rationalization.

Ask yourself the following questions:

- Does my phobia prevent me from enjoying other people?
- Does it prevent me from advancing in my career?
- Does it prevent me from enjoying activities that others find enjoyable?

If so, let go of your apathy, and start using the SKILL Tools. When Bob used them to overcome his agoraphobia, he realized that agoraphobia was a gift. If he had not had it, he would never have discovered Life Plus. We believe that you too will receive a bonus if you work to overcome your phobia. With the SKILL Tools you can get off the worry-go-round, overcome irrational fears, and find fulfillment.

CHAPTER 16

◆ ◆ ◆

Global Worries and the
Pathway to Life Plus

In this chapter we'd like to discuss the kind of problems that are not high on the lists of concerns reported by our focus groups, but which exist as low-grade, background fears that can intensify feelings of depression and helplessness. These are global concerns like the economy, the environment, crime, war, and incurable diseases. How can the SKILL Tools lessen worries of issues that affect the whole world?

"I feel as if our generation could be the one that destroys the earth because everyone is polluting and neglecting to care for the evironment," said one focus group member.

"It used to be safe to walk down my street at night, but now it's not. Crime is getting out of hand," said another.

Will our nation face another depression or another war? Will diseases like AIDS and drug addiction kill more and more people? And what can you, one person who has worries enough of her own, do about it? Can you bring peace and pure air to the world all by yourself? Can you rehabilitate or educate the masses? No, you can't, but you can join in humankind's greatest challenge. You can apply the SKILL Tools to global worries and free yourself of your fears. Then you can resolve to take one small action to make the world a better place. You can do the only thing you have responsibility for—using whatever gifts you have to contribute to the well-being of the planet. When you do that, you not only remove some of the clouds of negativity that keep humanity from feeling the healing rays of the sun, but you also learn to reach out to others, to give love and receive love, and to sense your own worthiness. You find Life Plus for yourself, even though the world is still not perfect. Global worries offer the perfect opportunity to pearl worry!

Our friend Jo McSherry is a good example of someone who has found Life Plus by doing what she is uniquely suited to do to affect a global concern. Jo spent several months caring for her brother, David Padgett, while he was dying from cancer. After his death, Jo was overcome with grief. To help herself recover, she enrolled in a class on attitudinal healing. Besides learning that it was normal to go through stages of anger, guilt, sadness, despair, and depression during grief, she learned how to go with her troubles, to accept herself and life as it was, and to live in the present moment. After the class was over, she looked for a support group for hurting people like herself. Finding none, she started her own. She began to reach out to AIDS patients who had a desperate need for attitudinal healing. Some of these dying friends reported feeling more alive than ever before, because they mastered attitudinal healing. Through her work, several families who were alienated from AIDS victims were reunited with their loved ones. Now she is planning a support group for family members.

Nearly everyone worries about AIDS, but Jo has done something about it. By taking action to heal herself emotionally, Jo has been able to help countless others. While Jo has always been a favorite of ours, she is now truly a special person in our estimation. She is bright, vibrant, and excited about life. She has obviously found Life Plus.

USING THE SKILL TOOLS
WITH GLOBAL ISSUES

When you use the First SKILL Tool to seek the real reason for your worry over global issues, it is easy to see that fear comes because you see yourself at the mercy of powerful forces that you perceive to be beyond your control. Psychologists tell us, however, that if you are able to take even a small amount of control over a worrisome situation, then your feeling of helplessness and worry diminishes. That is what Jo did and what you can do too. Use the Second SKILL Tool to brainstorm ways you can take action to alter global conditions. Here are some ideas about small things you can do to affect some prevalent global concerns:

• *The environment.* Stop using products in aerosol cans. Store food in reusable containers rather than plastic wrap. Switch from disposable to cloth diapers. Make sure your car engine is clean and that pollution-controlling devices work. Carpool or take public transportation whenever you can. Start an aluminum can recycling project at work.

• *Peace issues.* Start working for peace in your own personal life by reducing worries and letting go of unnecessary conflicts with others. Study international issues and be informed. Make your opinions known. Write your congressperson.

• *Crime and drug abuse.* Learn self-protection techniques. Organize neighborhood crime watch groups. Become informed about drugs. Support organizations that help abusers recover.

• *Incurable disease.* Know how to protect yourself. Educate your own family. Support research and caring organizations.

Undoubtedly you can think of many other small actions that you can take. Consider any special gifts you may have. Because Jane has recovered from cancer, she feels that she can relate effectively to others who are involved in trying to solve this global issue. She frequently volunteers to speak at American Cancer Society meetings, giving of her talents and of her special knowledge about cancer. Bob spends hours talking to people who have agoraphobia, motivating them to help themselves recover. Our National Professional Speakers Association is organizing a library of healing and inspirational books and tapes that will be lent to people who have catastrophic illnesses. Some of these books have been written by members themselves.

Next, use the Third SKILL Tool to image yourself successfully setting goals and taking action. Use the Fourth SKILL Tool to help you risk doing what you have imaged. Finally, use the Fifth SKILL Tool to let go of the concerns about which you can do nothing.

Once you become immersed in solutions, you will no longer think so much about the problems. By reaching out to others, even in a small way, you take control of your life. You can feel good about yourself because you are making your contribution to the universal solution for global worries. When billions of people do small things to solve a global issue, it will be solved—witness, for example, the destruction of the Berlin Wall in 1989.

THE IMPORTANCE OF ATTITUDE

Nancy Reuben Greenfield, executive director of Idealists International, believes that positive attitudes can be the beginning of the end for many global worries. This nonprofit organization started by her late father, Ed Reuben, functions like a support group for positive-thinking people with high ideals who believe in honest government and fair business practices, and who want to band together and make an impact on the world's problems.

"Sometimes it seems as if crime and corruption gang up against all the good people, and we wanted to offer a symbolic organization that functions to say it's okay to be honest, to be a good person. Idealists don't have a lot of organizational activities because they work in their own communities, doing things like feeding the hungry. By contributing to others, we help ourselves," she says.

Nancy believes everyone can take positive steps to stop worrying. We concur with her words of advice: "Do something for someone else. It doesn't have to be a big thing—you might just bring in your neighbor's newspaper when she's off on a trip, let someone go ahead of you into a lane of traffic, or spend a couple of hours on a rape crisis hotline. Once you give of yourself to someone else, you immediately feel better about yourself and you can stop worrying." The Idealists International's address is 2758 Keller Springs Road, Carrollton, Texas 75006, (214) 855-7684.

Our friend Judith Briles, a speaker and author, believes that sometimes traumatic events help you learn "not to sweat the small stuff." As a real estate developer and businesswoman, Judith had built her material assets to approximately $1 million in 1981. Then, in a partnership with another woman to build a small hotel, Judith raised more than $500,000 to buy property and augment the construction loan. Somehow most of the money "disappeared," and Judith was left holding the bag. After declaring bankruptcy, she was forced to sell all her assets including her home, cars, investments, and the remaining assets of her business to settle the claims.

Judith could have been bitter and given up, but she didn't. She discovered from her entrepreneurial women friends that many had been sabotaged in business by other women. This was a global problem, Judith felt, that went back at least as far as the days when Queen Elizabeth I used duplicity to undermine her cousin, Mary, Queen of Scots. Judith did research and published her conclusions in *Woman to Woman, From Sabotage to Support*. In it, she teaches women to benefit through mutual help and concern rather than destroying one another through sabotage. She is able to teach women to build confidence and believe in themselves because she has learned to believe in herself.

"I'm basically an optimistic person, but tragedy helped me realize what was important in life. In 1971 my baby died, and I learned that dusting and cleaning house weren't important. My remaining three children were. In the eighties, I lost a nineteen-year-old son and in addition went through the bankruptcy. I have had to learn to prioritize, and that is good. I don't consider myself a worrier and I'm not stuck in mediocrity like a lot of people," she said.

We believe that Judith has found Life Plus even though she has suffered much. Judith feels good about herself and doesn't worry because she takes actions on her own problems and helps others. Hers is a real success.

DISCOVERING THE BIG PICTURE

Jane says, "When we are immersed in our own fears and worries, we don't have a bigger, broader picture of the world and our connectedness with it. The clarity that comes from learning to become peaceful within ourselves, to live in the present moment, to solve our own problems, and to be assertive comes from using the SKILL Tools."

Bob says, "Peace in the world will come when we all learn to eliminate worry in our own lives. If enough people raise their consciousness about eliminating worry, we can start an epidemic of goodwill and positive action that will affect the universe."

If you want the peace that comes from not having to stew and fret and worry, from not having to lie awake at night or suffer headaches, backaches, and stomach upsets, from seeing only the penalty of your worry and not its pearl, then the SKILL Tools are for you. We hope that by using them, you will find your own unique gifts, and that when you discover them, you will pass them on to the world.

BIBLIOGRAPHY

◆ ◆ ◆

Adams, Jane. *Wake Up, Sleeping Beauty*. New York: William Morrow & Co., Inc., 1989.

The Aerobics Center. *Fit Tips*. 12330 Preston Road, Dallas, TX 75230, March 1989.

Alberti, Robert E., and Michael L. Emmons. *Your Perfect Right*. San Luis Obispo, CA: Impact Publishing Co., 1986.

American Heart Association. "Breaking Your Fast in a Healthy Way" *Heartstyle*, 11.

Bethel, Sheila Murray. *Making a Difference: The Twelve Qualities to Make You a Leader*. New York: Putnam, 1990.

Bettelheim, Bruno. *A Good Enough Parent*. New York: Alfred A. Knopf, 1987.

Blowers, Betty Sue, ed. *Bill Moyers: A World of Ideas*. New York: Doubleday, 1989.

Bradshaw, John. *Bradshaw On: The Family*. Health Communications, Inc., Pompano Beach, FL 33069, 1988.

Brans, J. *Take Two: True Stories of Real People Who Dared to Change Their Lives*. New York: Doubleday, 1989.

Briles, Judith. *The Confidence Factor*. New York: Master Media, 1990.

————*When God Says No*. Dallas: Word Publishing, 1990.

————*Woman to Woman: From Sabotage to Support*. Far Hills, NY: New Horizons Press, 1989.

Chopra, Deepak, M.D. *Quantam Healing*. New York: Bantam Books, 1989.

Claverlie, Laura. "Blue Moods." *Health*, September 1987.

Eron, C.. "Life Change: What Do Women Want?" *Science News*, July 1988.

Fensterheim, Herbert, Ph.D., and Jean Baer. *Don't Say Yes When You Want to Say No*. New York: Dell Publishing, 1978.

Gawain, Shakti. *Creative Visualization*. South Holland, IL: Bantam New Age, 1979.

Gibran, Kahlil. *The Prophet*. New York: Alfred A. Knopf, 1969.

Gullo, Stephen, Ph.D., and Connie Church. *Loveshock*. New York: Simon & Schuster, Inc., 1988.

Handly, Robert, and Pauline Neff. *Anxiety and Panic Attacks*. New York: Rawson Associates, 1985.

————*Beyond Fear.* New York: Rawson Associates, 1987.

Handly, Robert and Jane, and Pauline Neff. *The Life Plus Program For Getting Unstuck.* New York: Rawson Associates, 1989.

Hill, Napoleon. *Think and Grow Rich.* New York: Fawcett, 1960.

Kuehn, Paul. *Breast Care Options.* South Windsor, CT: Newmark Publishing Company, 1986.

Knipe, Wayne, *Better Grades Easier.* Janmore Group, P.O. Box 515992, Dallas 75251–5992, 1988.

Laws, J. L. "Psychology of Women: Future Directions in Research." *Psychological Dimensions,* 1978.

Leeds, Dorothy. *Smart Questions.* New York: McGraw Hill, 1987.

McAuliffe, Kathleen. "Prescription for a Healthy Old Age," *U.S. News & World Report,* 23 May 1988.

McDargh, Eilene. *How to Work for a Living and Still Be Free to Live.* San Diego: Loch Lomond Press, 1989.

McKay, Matthew, Ph.D., and Patrick Fanning. *Self-Esteem.* Oakland, CA: New Harbinger Publications, 1987.

Morris, Lois B. "Blue Moods." *Self,* April 1989.

Neff, Pauline. *Tough Love.* Nashville: Abingdon, 1982.

Payer, Lynn. *How to Avoid a Hysterectomy.* New York: Pantheon, 1987.

Restak, Richard. *The Brain: The Last Frontier.* New York: Doubleday, 1979.

Roane, Susan. *How to Work a Room.* New York: Shapolsky Press, 1988.

Scarf, Maggie. *Unfinished Business: Pressure Points in the Lives of Women.* New York: Ballantine, 1980.

Triere, Lynette. *Learning to Leave.* Chicago: Contemporary Books, 1982.

INDEX

♦ ♦ ♦